D0426499

The Clinton Syndrome

The President and the Self-Destructive Nature of Sexual Addiction

Jerome D. Levin, Ph.D.

FORUM

AN IMPRINT OF PRIMA PUBLISHING

In memory of my aunt Ella,
who taught me that sanity lies
in moderation.

© 1998 by Jerome D. Levin

All rights reserved. No part of this book may be reproduced or transmitted in any form or by any means, electronic or mechanical, including photo-copying, recording, or by any information storage or retrieval system, with-out written permission from Prima Publishing, except for the inclusion of quotations in a review.

Grateful acknowledgment is made to the following for permission to repro-duce previously published material: *Recovery from Alcoholism,* by Jerome D. Levin, Ph.D., Jason Aronson, Inc. Publishers. Copyright © 1991 by Jerome D. Levin.

FORUM
An imprint of Prima Publishing
3875 Atherton Road, Rocklin, CA 95765

PRIMA PUBLISHING and colophon are registered trademarks of Prima Communications, Inc.

Library of Congress Cataloging-in-Publication Data

Levin, Jerome D. (Jerome David)
    The Clinton syndrome : the president and the self-destructive nature of sexual addiction / Jerome D. Levin.
        p. cm.
    Includes bibliographical references and index.
    ISBN 0-7615-1628-X
    1. Clinton, Bill, 1946– —Sexual behavior. 2. Clinton, Bill, 1946–
—Psychology. 3. Presidents—United States—Biography. 4. Sex addiction—United States—Case studies. I. Title.
E886.2.L48 1998
973.929'092—dc21   98-18359
[B]   CIP

98 99 00 01 02 HH 10 9 8 7 6 5 4 3 2 1
Printed in the United States of America

HOW TO ORDER

Single copies may be ordered from Prima Publishing, P.O. Box 1260BK, Rocklin, CA 95677; telephone (916) 632-4400. Quantity discounts are also available. On your letterhead, include information concerning the intended use of the books and the number of books you wish to purchase.

Visit us online at www.primapublishing.com

CONCORDIA UNIVERSITY LIBRARY
PORTLAND, OR 97211

Those whom the gods would destroy,
they first make proud.

CONTENTS

Preface · vii

Introduction · 1

Part One A Psychological Portrait
of a Man Out of Control · 7

1. Irrationality in the Oval Office · 9

2. The Clinton Syndrome Explored · 23

3. Planting the Seeds of Addiction · 41

4. An Addiction Progresses · 69

5. The Master Seducer · 109

6. The Path to Self-Destruction · 129

Part Two Regaining Control:
The Recovery Process · 149

7. The Long, Difficult Road Back · 151

8. Step by Step · 177

9. Beyond the 12 Steps · 203

Afterword · 241

Bibliography · 245

Index · 247

CONTENTS

PREFACE

MY MAIN TASK IN this book is to define "sexual addiction" and demonstrate how President Clinton and his behavior typifies the definition. At the human level, an impaired president is no different from an impaired farmer or impaired vagrant. However, the national consequences of dysfunction in a politically powerful person such as Bill Clinton are vastly greater than the national consequences of the same dysfunction in a politically powerless person.

I am not an investigative reporter, a historian, or a political scientist. What I am is an addictions specialist who has spent the last quarter century treating a large number of men and women addicted to all kinds of things, ranging from crack cocaine to pain. In addition to my private practice, I have long taught students of alcoholism and substance-abuse counseling in a variety of settings. I now teach primarily at the New School for Social Research in Manhattan, where I serve as director of the Alcoholism and Substance Abuse Counselor Training Program.

I have a doctorate in rehabilitation counseling, which is one of the more practically oriented helping professions. It attempts, very directly, to help people recover from all kinds of disabilities, including addiction. This training has served me well. In 1981, I wrote my dissertation on personality change in men enrolled in Alcoholics Anonymous and ever since have been treating both chemical and behavioral addictions. I have also been trained in psychoanalysis, which I believe helps me understand the inner world—the *dynamics*—of people. This keeps me aware of the influence of the past on the present, of internal conflict, and of the importance of the patient's relationship to me.

Having said that I am not an investigative reporter or political scientist, you might wonder why I am writing a book about a political figure. The simplest reason is that it is hard not to. Although I have grown weary, along with the rest of the American public, of all the attention to the latest scandal about our president, there remains something compelling about the dilemma of Bill Clinton. The issue is too important—the mystery too deep—for me to leave it alone.

This country fascinates me. Although not my field of professional expertise, I have certainly not been indifferent to the political struggles of my generation. I love to read history and biography, and I am hung up on what the great jurist Oliver Wendell Holmes Jr. called "The American Experiment." In speaking of democracy, Holmes said, "It is an experiment, as all life is an experiment." The experiment, now more than 200 years old, has had all kinds of twists and turns, failures and triumphs. Clinton's presidency is another episode in that ongoing experiment. It may very well falter and fail because of a personal hang-up. This matters. It matters not only to Bill Clinton and his family but also to his political party, to his country, and to the world. We, as a people, have not always lived up to our ideals first articulated by our founding fathers, but these ideals matter—rhetoric matters. It is important that Jefferson, despite his having been a slaveholder, wrote the Declaration of Independence and not *Mein Kampf.* I have an emotional investment in the success of the American Experiment, and I care that a president's apparent personal pathology might damage that experimental process.

Accordingly, I am deeply interested in the motivations of this man. Assuming that the allegations are true, why would a man of Clinton's unquestionable intellect, breadth of knowledge, and clearly articulated commitment to our democracy put himself in a position of great vulnerability that may yet have fatal consequences for his presidency? That is a question worth answering.

In my clinical experience, I have found that sexual addiction is not only a real problem but that it is also surprisingly prevalent. Generally speaking, the people whom I have treated for sexual addiction came to see me for some other problem—frequently depression, alcoholism, or other substance abuse. Exactly how common is the problem? We don't really know because no solid statistics on sexual addiction exist. Part of the problem lies in the difficulty of defining "sexual addiction." The other part lies in the fact that people don't recognize their problem, feel deeply ashamed, or both and so are not readily forthcoming about their sexual behavior. Herein lies another motivation for my writing this book.

Preface

It is my hope that many of my readers will be either personally helped by this book or able to use the information and insight found within it to help someone they care about.

I would like to share the sources of my information about Bill Clinton. By far, the larger part of it has been absorbed, more or less automatically and unconsciously, over the last six years through reading the major newsmagazines and newspapers—especially *Time* and *Newsweek,* the *New York Times,* and the *Washington Post*—and watching the various national television news shows and talk shows—especially *Geraldo Rivera Live* and public television's *Charlie Rose.* I have not used anything in this book that was not widely reported as fact.

I have also drawn heavily on a number of biographies of our president. By far the most objective is *First in His Class,* by David Maraniss, a Pulitzer Prize–winning *Washington Post* reporter. He is especially sound on Clinton's formative years as a politician, as well as highly illuminating on Clinton's dysfunctional family background. *The Dysfunctional President,* by Paul Fick, goes into even more detail about the addictions in Clinton's family, especially the alcoholism of Clinton's stepfather and the cocaine addiction of Clinton's half-brother. *The Comeback Kid: The Life and Career of Bill Clinton,* by Charles Allen and Jonathan Portis, served as yet another source for my discussion. This fairly standard biography minimizes the problems in the president's life, though I still found it quite useful. I also consulted *Boy Clinton: The Political Biography,* by R. Emmett Tyrrell, Jr. Tyrrell is a witty and frequently vicious opponent who finds nearly everything that Clinton has done condemnable— he really hates the guy. However, he does have a lot of carefully documented material on Clinton's sex life and domestic life. Although I am aware that Tyrrell (to say the least) has an axe to grind, I found his observations about the Clintons persuasive. It would appear that using information from both Maraniss (pro-Clinton) and Tyrrell (anti-Clinton) probably balances out to form a reasonably accurate picture of the man.

Writing a psychobiography is notoriously tricky. I want to be very careful in impugning motivation— conscious or unconscious—to someone I don't know. Much of what I have to say about Clinton's motivations is based on fairly solid evidence. My other thoughts about him and what motivates his behaviors are derived from my knowledge of the addictions literature and my long experience with treating addiction. Someone once said that all worthwhile theorizing was tentative, provisional, and playful. I subscribe to that, so what I will have to say about President Clinton is offered in that spirit. I am aware that many of my conclusions about a public figure of whom I have no direct knowledge are hypotheses and therefore inferential. Nevertheless, given the media's in-depth reporting and the tremendous amount of information available on Clinton and his milieu, the kind of hypothesizing I am doing in this book is, I believe, entirely reasonable.

A word about my politics. My first political hero was Adlai Stevenson, so I guess that that tells you something about my position on the political spectrum. I voted for Bill Clinton twice, and I do not regret it. I strongly believe that misplaced prosecutory zeal that tramples on civil liberties and invades privacy is a far greater danger to the republic than is President Clinton's sexual practices, whatever they may be. So this book is not a hatchet job on Clinton—there is no lack of those. Rather, my intention is to look at Clinton's "problem" dispassionately, scientifically, and with empathy while, I must admit, being somewhat driven by anger at him for having put a political agenda that I support in jeopardy.

Throughout the book, you will find case histories of sex addicts. Although the identity of the people mentioned has been concealed by a variety of means, all the case vignettes have a basis in reality. Some of the figures are composites created much in the way a character in a novel might be created—out of the novelist's experience of several people. At times I incorporate aspects of my own experience or my own feelings, and in other cases I have simply changed the circumstances, age, location, and so on in such a way as to make identification of the originals well nigh impossible. However fictionalized the vignettes are, the emotional truth of the situations depicted in them remains intact. This is important because these stories will make real the nature of sexual addiction and the pain that accompanies it in a way that dispassionate scientific exposition cannot. Although our topic is a serious one, I believe that humor has its uses, and I remind my readers that I am never laughing at the people but at their foibles and at the absurdities that people get themselves into. These unidentifiable yet real characters are intended to bring to life what it's like to have a sexual addiction, to struggle against it, and in some cases to recover from it.

I WOULD LIKE TO thank Karen Naungayan and Lorna Dolley for their very hard work on the manuscript.

I would also like to express my gratitude to the Riverhead, New York public library and its reference desk, which helped me search the professional literature on sexual addiction and provided me with almost instant reprints of the articles I wished to read. Similar help was forthcoming from the reference staff of the Fogelman library of the New School for Social Research. I am equally grateful for their assistance. However, my greatest debt is to my patients, who have taught me so much about addiction, and to my students, who over a span of many years have provided me an unequaled opportunity to test out my ideas about addiction.

INTRODUCTION

THIS IS A BOOK about a man and a problem, a president and a syndrome. The man is Bill Clinton, President of the United States, and the problem is sexual addiction. I attempt to determine, without personally knowing the man, the degree to which the president suffers from this condition. This is a risky endeavor at best but one that I believe is worth doing. The public domain contains an enormous amount of information from which I have drawn to try to reach a balanced appraisal of what demons drive this man. Those same demons drive every one of us. Sometimes we harness them more successfully than at other times, and some of us do a better job of it than others, but all human beings struggle with mastering their drives, including their sexual drive.

Sexual addiction affects a large number of people. It ruins family life, destroys careers, spreads disease, and makes those who suffer from it miserable, yet it is the one addiction that has not come out of the closet, because there is too much shame attached to it. Aside from examining the addictive behaviors of President Clinton, I hope that this book will also contribute to public awareness and reach sex addicts and their families.

Sexual addictions are not about sex. They are about insecurity, low self-esteem, and the need for affirmation

1

and reassurance. At the bottom, the sex addict feels unloved and unlovable and so looks obsessively for proof that this is not so. This is the case regardless of how skillfully the addict disguises his feelings of worthlessness from himself and from the world. Sexual addiction is an illness, and its sufferers deserve our compassion and empathy.

No one doubts that Bill Clinton has had an active extramarital sex life. In various ways, he himself has admitted as much. The question is: Is this "normal" human behavior in a powerful, high-energy, handsome male? Is it a character defect? Is it an addiction? This book attempts to answer these difficult questions.

Both the man and the problem are extraordinarily complex. President Clinton is brilliant, well educated, and informed; a voracious reader who forgets nothing that he has read; a consummate politician; a superb communicator; and a man of vast charm. Yet, for all these impressive assets, he is perceived as devious and dishonest and as having integrity, character, and zipper problems. Is President Clinton all of these, none of these, or, as is probable, a bewildering mix of assets and liabilities, of strengths and weaknesses? As difficult as it is for some of us, the citizens who twice elected him to the highest office in the land, to integrate the two Clintons, imagine what it must be like for the president himself to try to integrate these conflicting aspects of who he is.

All human beings are complex. Few function consistently in different situations, in different roles, in different areas of life, and at different periods in life. The degree to which people can make any sense to themselves or to others varies widely. In Clinton's case, the inner conflict and inconsistency appear to be extreme, but even more extreme is the conflict between his public presentation in the various masks he assumes and his inner being.

As we will see, the problem is also very complex. Sexuality is a mystery. Its dark yet wonderful power provides some of the best moments in life while confusing, compelling, conflicting, and tormenting. Human beings, everywhere and at all times, have struggled to define their sexual selves and their culture's standards of sexual behavior. Such efforts have not been entirely successful, regardless of culture, religion, or the individual. Sex is baffling. It is too powerful, too wonderful, too strongly driven, and too tinged with shame and guilt for most of us to be entirely comfortable with our sexual selves.

Writing about sex is tricky. It is all too easy to be puritanical, and it is just as easy to be preachy. I wish to be neither. Nor do I want to be judgmental under the guise of being scientific, using the notion of sexual addiction as a stick to whip Clinton. In trying to avoid these dangers, I have kept in mind the great psychoanalyst Eric Erikson's distinction between the *moral* and the *ethical* as written in *Gandhi's Truth*, a magnificent study of the Indian leader. For Erikson, the moral is the unconscious, driven, harsh judgmental part of us that condemns self and others. It is the voice of the past within us—automatic and unthinking. It seeks to blame and is essentially irrational.

As a psychoanalyst would say, it is the stuff of the super-ego (the unconscious judge within). It is what the philosopher Friedrich Nietzsche spoke of when he said, "Morality is resentment."

The ethical, on the other hand, comes from that part of us that tries to find a just, sane, balanced way of living together harmoniously. It is conscious, it tries to be rational, and it seeks to find understanding and make behavioral choices in full knowledge of the complexity of reality. It does not condemn self or others. A psychoanalyst would say that it is the stuff of the ego (the rational part of the mind). In this book, I have tried to approach the issue from the standpoint of the ethical, not the moral, and to make this a work of the ego, not the superego.

President Clinton is no different from the rest of us in having to struggle throughout his life to find sexual satisfaction, to renounce some sexual desires, and to control his sexual appetite. Yes, Clinton is a man, a human being like all of us, but he is also a president, so he is both the same and different. His sexual conflicts and what he does with them matter more in the sense that they affect the destiny of a nation and indeed the entire world in a way in which most of our sexual choices, behaviors, conflicts, and joys simply do not.

The notion that Clinton is a sex addict and that his extramarital activities have been intense, numerous, and varied is not new. Commentators as ideologically different as Pulitzer Prize–winning Clinton biographer David Maraniss, *New York Times* columnist A. M. Rosenthal, Stanford University professor of psychiatry Alvin Cooper, feminist Gloria Steinem, best-selling author Wendy Kaminer, and the Reverend Jerry Falwell have suggested that if the allegations are true, Bill Clinton is a sex addict.

This book does not attempt to answer *what* Clinton did. In fact, the picture of Clinton and the psychological hypotheses about him that I draw are based on the *assumption* that the sexual allegations are true. This assumption is one that every poll shows is shared by the majority of my fellow citizens and has a great deal of evidence to support it. Of course, the president has denied the allegations, but he has done so in such a way that most commentators have thought his denial equivocal. The vast majority of these commentators have believed that these allegations are true.

In this book, I will argue that Clinton's background as a child of addiction predisposed him biologically and socially to an addiction of his own. I will demonstrate that his sexual proclivities over a lifetime were expansive and developed the strength and persistence of a habit. Finally, I will illustrate that there were specific stresses in the president's life shortly before his alleged involvement with Monica Lewinsky that made him highly vulnerable to acting out once again his sexually addictive behavior.

I ask you to try to identify with Bill Clinton, not in the particulars of his addictive behavior but in your own addictive behaviors and activities, those that sometimes cause you to feel out of control. We all have them. Try to feel how dangerous it is to be out of control and then speculate about why you might be out of control. You will learn a lot.

The Monica Lewinsky story and all of its spin-offs is a rapidly unfolding drama. Each day brings new revelations and new speculations. I am sure that more rumors, spins, and hard facts will continue to emerge. However, I do not believe that future public details of the president's sex life will change my theory about Clinton and his sexual problem.

The conclusion of all of this is that you, the reader of this book, are going to know and to note things that I, the writer, cannot as they surface over the ensuing months. Regardless, I will maintain my thesis that the president's sexual proclivities not only serve as a paradigm of sexually addictive behavior but also have profound ramifications for the well-being of our nation.

PART ONE

A Psychological Portrait of a Man Out of Control

CHAPTER ONE

Irrationality
in the Oval Office

ILL CLINTON IS HARDLY the first political leader to be caught up in a sexual scandal. From Cleopatra and Mark Antony to Kitty O'Shea and Charles Stewart Parnell, the fates of empires have turned on the private passions of their leaders. Antony's lust for Cleopatra cost him the Roman Empire, whereas Parnell's passion for Mrs. O'Shea cost the Irish their strongest leader and probably delayed for a generation their liberation from English rule. There have been legions of autocratic, decadent, licentious rulers. Clement VII, the Renaissance pope, had a relationship with a woman such that she was his daughter (by birth), daughter-in-law (by marriage to his son), and mother of his child; Franklin Roosevelt had a 30-year affair with Lucy Mercer Rutherford; and John Kennedy had one with Marilyn Monroe.

Therefore, the intrusion of private sexual conduct into the realm of the public and political is hardly news. However, there is something different about President Clinton's sexuality and the political ramifications of that sexuality. It appears that it is neither the grand passion of a Mark Antony or a Parnell nor the overripe decadence of a Renaissance pope nor the longtime love of an essentially lonely man. Rather, it is something quite different: the irrational behavior of a basically decent middle-class democratic leader, behavior that may have tragic consequences for both the man and the nation.

When the country learned that tapes existed of former White House intern Monica Lewinsky discussing her sexual relationship with President Clinton after he had denied having had sex with her, there was a sense of shock. First Lady Hillary Clinton, true to form, quickly came to her husband's defense, asserting his innocence and the existence of a vast right-wing conspiracy aimed at her husband and herself. However, the tapes that might contradict the president's story had already fallen into the hands of Special Prosecutor Kenneth Starr, and talk of impeachment arose. It appeared that Clinton, in testifying in the Paula Jones suit that he had not had sex with Lewinsky and in allegedly urging Lewinsky to lie about their relationship, was guilty of at least perjury and likely obstruction of justice as well. Although most Americans thought that the president's sex life, like their own, should be a private matter, they felt *betrayed*. During the 1992 presidential election, Clinton first denied having had an affair with Gennifer Flowers yet more or less admitted it on national television when he gave an interview to *60 Minutes*. During that interview, Clinton stated that he and Hillary had had marital difficulties but that they had overcome them and that their marriage was stronger than ever. Essentially, Clinton had promised to straighten up in the White House. Suddenly, that did not appear to be the case.

After the initial sense of shock, public reaction ranged from rage to hurt to amusement to indifference to joy (on the part of Clinton's enemies). Despite the multitude of emotions felt, the public shared one common thought: *Why would Bill Clinton do something so stupid?* Why would he put his historical role in jeopardy?

What was your initial reaction? Mine was one of anger. I remember asking, "Why did he play into the hands of the most destructive elements in American politics?" My reaction began to temper, however, as I realized that Bill Clinton was exhibiting the symptoms of someone in the grip of an untreated addiction. Had the Monica Lewinsky affair been an isolated event, it would have appeared to have been a single case of marital infidelity, and I never would have entertained the thought of "Clinton as a sex addict." However, the Monica Lewinsky affair was *not* an isolated event, and the more I thought about it, the more I realized that Clinton had about as much chance of leaving her alone as a cocaine addict has of passing up a line.

As I stated in the introduction, *sexual addictions are not about sex*. They are about insecurity, low self-esteem, and the need for affirmation and reassurance. The sex addict feels unloved and unlovable and therefore looks obsessively for proof that this is not so. The sex addict disguises his feelings of worthlessness from himself and from the world. The sex addict uses sex to deaden and avoid psychological pain and conflict, reassure and bolster fragile self-esteem, and bury deeply embedded feelings of self-hatred.

Monica Lewinsky was only 21 when Bill Clinton's sexual relationship with her began, and the contrast in power between them was striking. Not only did the age difference contribute to this power differential, but the vast disparity between their respective ranges of experience and their status as intern and president, respectively, made this little better than "robbing the cradle." It was a tawdry business at best, one of secret sex with a young student, perhaps literally behind a stack of state papers.

Clinton knew that both the special prosecutor and Paula Jones's attorneys were scrutinizing his behavior in microscopic detail. Given this, and in the absence of an addiction, his relationship with Lewinksy would make no sense whatsoever, unless he be regarded as self-destructive to the point of madness. However, I do not believe that Clinton is self-destructive. People who will their own downfall may not be aware of the destructive nature of their actions, however, to an outside observer, the destructiveness may be readily apparent. Nothing in Clinton's background, history, or life up to the Lewinsky incident indicates that he is a man who is his own worst enemy in any *motivated* sense. In other words, Clinton's behavior may indeed lead to his destruction, but that destruction is not the motive for his actions. President Richard Nixon, another extraordinarily complex public figure, provides a ready contrast. You could feel the man sharpening the knife with which his enemies would slit his throat. Nixon's self-destructiveness was manifest in his self-pity ("You won't have Nixon to kick around anymore"), in his clumsy attempts to cover up, and most spectacularly in recording evidence of his own guilt and not destroying the incriminating tapes when he still could do so with impunity. It was as if Nixon clung to the tapes in order to destroy himself. Little evidence exists for anything of this sort in Clinton's life. Clinton is a man driven to succeed, to climb the ladder, to go from triumph to triumph.

I believe that a case can be made that the Lewinsky affair resulted from a mix of *many* factors. Remember: Clinton's affair with Lewinsky was not primarily about sex. Rather, it was about an insecure man seeking reassurance and validation of his worth.

The first and most important factor that drove Clinton toward Monica Lewinsky was his history of having been raised in a violently alcoholic, dysfunctional home. Studies have shown that predisposition to addictive behavior is partly biological and partly environmental. Exactly what goes into the mix is debated by scientists, but no one in the field of addiction—researcher or clinician— doubts that addiction in the family powerfully predisposes children to addiction. I will postpone my discussion of the role of violence in addiction and its consequences for children and simply note that Clinton was witness to such violence at an early age. I know, from many years of practice, that the consequences of such an upbringing are indelible. Only with extensive treatment do people overcome the legacy of such childhoods. Although Clinton has, by the world's standards, done extremely well, the external achievement does not heal the inner devastation.

The second factor was Clinton's previous record of infidelity. His affair with Lewinsky has many antecedents. As far back as his first campaign for public office in 1974, when he ran for the U.S. Congress shortly after receiving his law degree, his reputation for philandering was such that Hillary, at that point engaged to Bill, sent her father and brother ostensibly to work in his campaign. It was common knowledge, however, that they were there to spy on Bill, who already had two girlfriends on the side. Clinton lost that election but went on to become attorney general of Arkansas in 1976. Bill and Hillary had married in 1975, and by this time (according to all of Clinton's biographers) the allegations of sexual misconduct on Bill's part became routine and expected. By the time Clinton met Lewinsky, he had developed a lifetime habit of taking sexual pleasures wherever they could be found. Old habits are hard to break, and Bill Clinton is no exception to the rule.

The third factor was the two-year period during which Clinton suffered three major losses. His mother, Virginia Kelly, died on January 6, 1994; Israeli Prime Minister Yitzhak Rabin, an important father figure to

Clinton, was assassinated on November 4, 1995; and U.S. Commerce Secretary and friend Ron Brown was killed in a plane crash on April 3, 1996. Clinton was muted in his public sorrow for his mother but not for the two men.

Clinton's loss of his mother, although perhaps both privately and deep within his psyche the most wounding of his losses, is the one that elicited the least public expression of emotion. This is puzzling, for Clinton is, by nature, an emotionally expressive man. This unexpected lack of emotion suggests deep and strongly conflicted feelings about his mother. Whatever the nature of that conflict, Clinton's attachment to her is manifest and documented by all his biographers, both friendly and unfriendly. Clinton's mother was a strong, flamboyant, extroverted gambler and lady-about-town, and she had a reputation as a "flirt." This certainly suggests that Clinton's sexual proclivities may stem, at least in part, from his identification with his mother. This identification may be a conscious modeling of his mother or, as is far more likely, an unconscious reenactment of her traits and behaviors. For all his attachment, Clinton had mixed feelings about his high-flying, wide-ranging mother. Such ambivalence—simultaneous feelings of love and of hate—impede mourning and therefore make moving on with one's life more difficult.

Clinton's experiences with father figures have been filled with tragedy. His biological father, William Jefferson Blythe, was killed in a car accident before Clinton was born; his stepfather, Roger Clinton, was a violent drunk; and there have been a long series of surrogate fathers who either failed him, died, or became unavailable to him. Clinton's ongoing search for a father likely has been one of the strongest motivators in his life.

The assassination of Rabin, which might have derailed the Middle East peace process (to which Clinton is deeply committed), rendered Clinton helpless, and it was as though fate had derailed his plans to go down in history as a peacemaker. The president was appalled by both the fanaticism of the assassin and the assassin's cause. It is not surprising that Clinton would be extraordinarily distraught by both the loss of an admired ally and his natural identification with the assassination of a political leader. Nevertheless, Clinton's reaction was so overtly emotional (he almost lost composure at Rabin's funeral) and so deeply felt that some additional factor must have been at work. Clearly, his relationship with Rabin had some further deep and personal meaning to him.

As numerous commentators wrote at the time of Rabin's death, when the intensity of Clinton's reaction was being widely commented on, Rabin had been not only an important father figure to Clinton but also a famous warrior who had manifested the kind of courage in battle that Clinton's draft evasion had prevented him from claiming for himself. Additionally, Rabin had accepted Clinton and did not criticize Clinton's behavior during the Vietnam War. Rabin, though not an alcoholic, was known to be a heavy drinker, so Clinton had found a father who could drink yet function—and function magnificently—the exact opposite of Clinton's pathetically alcoholic stepfather. Rabin was a man's man who had not only physical but moral courage, a trait to which

Clinton aspired and was frequently condemned for lacking. Rabin and Clinton had become allies in a supremely important quest: to bring peace to the Middle East. All these factors made Rabin an almost perfect father surrogate for President Clinton. Anyone watching the video of Clinton at Rabin's funeral would be unable to deny his devastation. This was a loss that really stunned him. Rabin was the last in a long series of father surrogates in Clinton's life, and his passing left Clinton vulnerable. A hole needed to be filled, one that could not be filled by another surrogate father. This was one loss too many, and it became unlikely that Clinton would risk—on any level, conscious or unconscious—becoming that emotionally tied to a "father" again.

Having lost his mother and the last of his fathers, both real and surrogate, Clinton truly was an orphan. Then came another devastating blow: the loss of an older-brother figure, friend, and political ally, Ron Brown. Clinton was again extremely emotional in his public reaction to Brown's death. Dying in a plane crash is both sudden and unexpected and, in this manner, not much different from dying in a car crash. Therefore, Brown's tragic death had to have brought to mind Clinton's biological father's equally tragic death. Although Clinton expressed deep emotion over the losses of Rabin and Brown, the pace of public life left him no time to "work through" these losses and complete the mourning process. I am suggesting that Clinton was reeling under the impact of three profound losses, each imperfectly and incompletely mourned.

The fourth factor was Bill Clinton's beleaguered presidency during the Republican sweep of Congress in 1994 and the country's subsequent turn to the right. These actions marginalized him and robbed him of much of his leadership role—again another major loss. However, the 1996 presidential campaign was made easier by the nomination of a weak Republican candidate, Bob Dole, and a third-party candidate lacking credibility, Ross Perot. Clinton displayed political genius and turned the tide on his opponents.

Things were beginning to look better for Clinton, but with his political resurrection came a different kind of emotional danger. Having pulled the chestnuts from the ashes in an extraordinary way, he was suddenly in a strong leadership position despite the opposition party's control of Congress. He now had ample proof that the American people supported him, however tempered that approval was by a lack of confidence in Dole and Perot. Clinton was insecurely, yet strongly, in the driver's seat again. The danger now lay in whether this renewed position of power would feed his grandiosity and lead him to behave recklessly. Would newfound arrogance, overconfidence, and overweening pride (covering his abysmally low self-esteem) lead him into reckless actions because he believed that he was invulnerable? Here is yet a fifth factor, feeding yet another stream into the river that would sweep him into Monica Lewinsky's arms. It has been said, and wisely so, that "Those whom the Gods would destroy, they first make proud." Clinton's political comeback might have done exactly that by increasing his vulnerability to reckless sexual behavior.

A predisposition to addiction, a lifetime behavioral pattern of infidelity, three deep and devastating losses, and a political comeback engendering arrogance all pulled Bill Clinton in the direction of Monica Lewinsky. What happened after that was circumstance.

There is an interesting photograph of Virginia Kelly (Clinton's mother) and William Jefferson Blythe (Clinton's biological father) in the archives of the *Washington Post* (reproduced as photograph 2 in David Maraniss's biography of Clinton, *First in His Class*). Kelly looks extraordinarily like Lewinsky. Kelly's hairstyle, heavy makeup, and the overall impression are strikingly similar to Lewinsky's. Bill Clinton, the man who had lost his mother, had found a replacement for her. Whatever Oedipal longings Clinton may have had toward his overtly sexual mother may have been fulfilled with a woman who somewhat resembles his mother. Of course, I cannot know what was in Clinton's mind, conscious or unconscious, or whether he ever made such a connection, but the resemblance is noteworthy nonetheless.

Now there is no mystery to why Bill Clinton would have gotten into a virtually suicidal relationship with Monica Lewinsky. His legacy as an adult child of an alcoholic (ACOA) compelled him to fill the emptiness of his childhood and to repeat the addictive pattern of both his biological and his adoptive parents; his relationship with

Lewinsky revived a longstanding behavioral pattern; she fulfilled a complex nexus of unconscious needs—needs that were exacerbated by the loss of three important figures in his life; he derived reassurance when his political fortunes were in doubt and then continued to pursue that reassurance with a grandiose recklessness once the pendulum had swung; and last, but not least, she was there, and she was available. Absent any insight into what he was doing, he had no choice but to fall into a really stupid trap.

Clinton has bared his throat to a hoard of savage enemies led by the special prosecutor for the sake of an apparently meaningless relationship with Lewinsky. A man of acute political awareness, Clinton surely heard the baying hounds at heel, yet he stumbled (how close we do not yet know) toward their jaws. In making himself vulnerable to devastating disclosure, public scrutiny, and persecutory zeal, he endangered not only his presidency and place in history but also the political agenda (of moderation, tolerance, and the pursuit of peace) to which he appears sincerely committed. To do this for the sake of having oral sex bespeaks of either recklessness bordering on madness—a recklessness beyond that associated with grandiosity—which simply is not Clinton, or the irrationally compulsive behavior of an addict seeking affirmation and reassurance.

Assuming that President Clinton did half the sexual things he is alleged to have done, he has undoubtedly lost control—to be specific, he has become powerless over his sexual impulses. Although it now seems unlikely (although not impossible) that Clinton's relationship with Lewinsky will result in his impeachment, his reputation is indelibly stained.

CHAPTER TWO

The Clinton Syndrome Explored

.M. ROSENTHAL, THE renowned *New York Times* editor and columnist, has suggested, "For President Clinton to have elicited sex in the Oval Office would have been like doing it in Macys's window . . . and for him to take that risk could mean that he is obsessive, something like a sexual kleptomaniac." What an interesting analogy. Kleptomaniacs are unable to control their impulses; they see something that they want, and they grab it. Additionally, kleptomaniacs do not steal items because they need them. For example, if they steal food, it is not because they are hungry. Rather, it's the *feeling* that comes from the stealing—the very illicitness of the acquisition—that serves as the main kick. Likewise (to use Rosenthal's notion), a sexual kleptomaniac would be unable to control his or her impulses and would not have sex because he or she was horny. Rather, the thrill of getting away with something illicit would serve as the main kick. The notion of "sexual kleptomania" provides a good way of looking at Clinton's behavior and a simple way to understand the complex issues I will address in this book. Unwittingly perhaps, Rosenthal at once articulated the thought on everyone's mind and provided a solid psychological explanation for Clinton's behavior.

The very concept of sexual addiction is fraught with controversy and no small degree of skepticism on the part of many. However, it is not a new idea, and the vast amount of sexual addiction literature strongly attests to the fact that the problem is now becoming widely recognized. First, Amazon.com, the online book retailer, offers at least 50 titles specific to sexual addiction, including four titles by Patrick Carnes, Ph.D., clinical director of the Program for Sexual Dependency and Sexual Trauma in Torrance, California. Carnes is the psychologist who put sexual addiction on the map, having written numerous books on the subject, including *Out of the Shadows: Understanding Sexual Addiction* and *Don't Call It Love: Recovery from Sexual Addiction*. Second, the existence and proliferation of support groups such as Sex Addicts Anonymous, Sexual Compulsives Anonymous, Sex and Love Addicts Anonymous, and Sexaholics Anonymous demonstrates the pervasiveness of the problem and provides compelling evidence that this is a real and problematic entity. Third, the formation of organizations such as the National Council on Sexual Addiction and Compulsivity and the

Sexual Recovery Institute further attests to the existence of sexual addiction as a recognizable problem. In fact, even the National Institutes of Health has identified sexual addiction as a "research priority."

Therefore, it is not my goal in this book to prove that sexual addiction exits. It does. There is a wealth of research, compelling data, and case histories that allow us to accept it as a viable diagnosis and certain behavior. It is necessary, however, to elucidate the problem and explain how one goes about making such an assessment. This chapter looks at the psychological foundation for sexual addiction and introduces the criteria that clinicians commonly apply when diagnosing a sexually addicted individual.

The American Psychiatric Association (APA) publishes the mental health profession's authoritative, clinical reference manual—the *Diagnostic and Statistical Manual (DSM)*. The *DSM* is used by psychiatrists, psychologists, and all other professionals in the mental health field. Since 1952 it has been the most comprehensive psychiatric compendium available, describing criteria and clinical diagnoses for myriad disorders, including those related to anxiety, mood, substance abuse, development, and all major psychiatric illnesses.

Psychiatric diagnosis is a fallible business—not because diseases come into (and go out of) being but because our perceptions and therefore our evaluations of psychiatric disease change. The APA's definition of and criteria for the various psychiatric (emotional) illnesses have likewise changed and continue to change as new editions of the *DSM* are published. For example, some disease entities appear in the fourth edition (*DSM-IV*) that were not in the third (*DSM-III*), and some that appeared in the third edition were deleted from the fourth.

Defining *addiction* has baffled clinicians and researchers for a long time. Interestingly, the current *DSM* edition, *DSM-IV*, does not contain a definition or diagnosis for "sexual addiction." In fact, the *DSM-IV* does not have a category for "addiction" as a diagnosis at all; rather, it speaks of *substance abuse* and *substance dependence*. Therefore, mental health professionals treating drug and alcohol "addicts" classify their patients using diagnostic criteria from a combination of these two categories.

Although the criteria for each somewhat overlap, the two are distinguished by their degree of severity. Substance abuse is less severe than substance dependence, because abuse is the natural and necessary precursor to dependence—one cannot become *dependent* on a substance without having first *abused* the substance. Therefore, addicts both abuse and depend on their substance of choice.

Although these categories apply to substances, such as alcohol or drugs, many mental health professionals have expanded these categories to apply to behaviors as well. The Sexual Recovery Institute, a Los Angeles–based special therapy agency, acknowledges, "Addiction is a concept that traditionally was applied only to out-of-control use of alcohol and other drugs. Now, however, the term *addiction* is routinely used to describe and diagnose behaviors such as gambling, overeating, and sex when they are out of control." So, to create our working definition of sexual addiction, we must use the notion of substance addiction while keeping in mind that the "substance," for our purposes, is "sex."

The following list represents an adaptation of the *DSM* diagnostic criteria. These criteria manifest in people who suffer from sexual addiction. Each will be further explained in the text that follows:

1. Repeated sexual activity resulting in a failure to fulfill major role obligations at work, school, or home.

2. Sexual activity in potentially dangerous situations.

3. Repeated sex-related legal problems.

4. Continued sexual activity despite persistent or recurrent social or interpersonal problems.

5. Tolerance.

6. Withdrawal.

7. Larger amounts of sexual activity over longer periods of time than originally intended.

8. An enduring desire to control sexual activity and simultaneous failed attempts to do so.

9. Increased time spent in activities necessary to obtain sexual activity and/or to recover from its effects.

10. Decreased social, occupational, or recreational activities directly related to sexual activity.

11. Continued sexual activity despite knowledge of persistent or recurrent physical or psychological problems that are caused or exacerbated by the activity.

Repeated sexual activity resulting in a failure to fulfill major role obligations at work, school, or home.

For sex addicts, the addictive behavior can certainly affect work- or school-related obligations, but it most commonly affects one's obligations at home.

John was the manager of a support service department at a research facility. He was known to be tyrannical and to engage in bizarre acts such as lighting matches to papers on his subordinates' desks. He also habitually hit on lower-level employees, especially the secretaries. Because he "produced," his behavior was ignored by his superiors until his suggestive verbal advances progressed to groping. The subsequent demoralization within his department resulted in faltering productivity, and as a result he was dismissed. In John's case, the failure to fulfill a major role obligation was most manifest in the workplace.

Sexual activity in potentially dangerous situations.

The sex addicts with whom I have worked have, without exception, engaged in sex despite dangerous risks. Their compulsion commonly resulted in having unprotected sex, during which they repeatedly risked contracting sexually transmitted diseases and human immunodeficiency virus (HIV).

Additionally, because most sex addicts engage in sex with complete strangers, many risk ending up in unsafe places where, should danger arise, no help is available. I have treated many addicts who have been "roughed up." Larry, a gay sex addict, came close to being killed by two "gay bashers" he had picked up. He is now permanently physically disabled and walks only with difficulty and with the aid of mechanical appliances, yet even this event failed to keep him from engaging in more addictive behavior. The risk of getting "caught in the act" also constitutes a danger. For example, I've treated addicts who have had sex in public parks located in the middle of a busy city. Despite such dangers, addicts' desires for new conquests become so strong that outrageous risks are repeatedly taken and then bemoaned.

Repeated sex-related legal problems.

Many sex addicts expose themselves to blackmail, put themselves in positions to be financially castrated by vengeful spouses, and risk civil (and sometimes even criminal) proceedings as a result of their sexual behavior. Despite these consequences, they continue to behave in the same way.

Nancy's husband was hell-bent on proving her an unfit mother and gaining custody of their children. Yet, despite knowing that her husband had her apartment under surveillance, she brought home a seemingly endless stream of men. So addicted was she to sex that she lost custody of her children.

Continued sexual activity despite persistent or recurrent social or interpersonal problems.

If the addiction is marked and advanced, nearly every sex addict suffers social or interpersonal problems. This is because addictions invade every aspect of life. Despite these problems, however, addicts continue to engage in the addictive behavior.

Harry sincerely loved his wife and repeatedly told her so, yet he always had to have some "action on the side." Because Harry was not a skillful liar, eventually his wife learned of the affairs. This led to violent fights at home and the suffering and depression of the wife he loved. As a result, Harry suffered intensely from guilt. Even still, he could not alter his behavior.

Tolerance, as evidenced by either of the following:
(a) Needing increased amounts of sexual activity to achieve the high or the desired effect.

Some sex addicts become compelled to engage in increasingly frequent encounters to achieve the same effect. That effect, on a conscious level, is sexual pleasure; however, and more important, on an unconscious level, the effect is an emotional one, such as warding off depression, feelings of inadequacy, or loneliness. Just as the drinker must drink increasingly more to get the effects of alcohol, the sex addict needs to increase the amount of sexual activity to achieve the same desired effect of meeting the unconscious emotional need.

(b) A markedly diminished response to the same amount of sexual activity.

Eugene O'Neill's 1940 play *The Iceman Cometh* deals with the issue of alcoholism. A group of skid row bums are hanging around Harry Hope's dead-end saloon when Hickey, a traveling salesman, arrives for his annual visit. The rummies are in a state of great excitement because Hickey always pays for drinks while he is staying at Harry Hope's. However, this year Hickey has been transformed—he is on the wagon and preaching temperance. The denizens of Harry Hope's are appalled. Despite all Hickey's preaching, he continues to pay for the men's drinks; however, the alcohol no longer has an effect on the men—the booze just doesn't work anymore. Throughout the play is a haunting refrain, almost like that of a Greek chorus: "Harry, what have you done with the booze, it doesn't have the old magic anymore." This same idea applies to sexual activity that loses its so-called magic. When the same amount of sexual activity no longer has the power to temporarily fill the emotional void of the addict, a tolerance has indeed been built.

John, the manager who set fire to his employees' desks and hit on department secretaries, well illustrates the notion of escalation. When verbal harassment no longer satisfied him, he moved on to groping and was subsequently fired.

Joey was once satisfied with his nightly practice of "turning a trick." Soon, however, he was no longer satisfied with just one, and after finishing with his first trick, he had to return to the bar for one more "conquest." Eventually, he experienced such a lack of satisfaction that no matter how many times he scored, he returned home depressed.

Withdrawal, as evidenced by either of the following:
(a) Withdrawal symptoms characteristic for (addictive) sexual activity.

Sex addicts may experience all the psychological symptoms of substance withdrawal: anxiety, irritability, anger, depression, restlessness, insomnia, and mood swings. However, unlike the physiological symptoms of substance withdrawal, the psychological symptoms of withdrawal from sexual addiction are not physically dangerous. Therefore, although no one will die from the withdrawal symptoms associated with sexual addiction, individuals may *feel* so miserable that they wish they would die.

(b) Use of sexual activity, or similar compulsive behavior, to alleviate or avoid withdrawal symptoms.

The use of sexual activity to alleviate or avoid the aforementioned withdrawal symptoms has been reported in studies conducted by Dr. Wayne Meyers, professor of psychiatry at Columbia University Medical School. Dr. Meyers believes that many (if not most) sex addicts use sex as an antidepressant. In this way, they ward off the withdrawal symptoms of depression and even anxiety, irritability, anger, and mood swings and set up a vicious cycle in which they return to sex to escape from the withdrawal symptoms that are exacerbated if and when the addict stops the addictive behavior. Sex addicts commonly turn to other compulsive activities (such as gambling) or to substances to hold their potential withdrawal symptoms at bay.

Larger amounts of sexual activity over longer periods than originally intended.

Carrie's addictive pursuit of sex partners prevented her from working on the novel she was writing. Her addiction invaded more and more of her life until she literally had no time for anything else. She needed to be engaged in sex—looking for it, having it, or recovering from it—to the exclusion of all else.

An enduring desire to control sexual activity and simultaneous failed attempts to do so.

I regularly hear statements like the following from sex addicts: "I was going to work yesterday and I swore I wasn't going into the park to cruise, yet I somehow ended up there. I don't even remember walking into the park, but the next thing I knew I was behind some bushes engaged in oral sex. I enjoyed it, but I was furious at myself. I was not only late for work again, but it just wasn't what I had wanted to do."

Susan, one of my patients, liked to go out dancing. Her husband rationalized that even though she went out three, four, and sometimes even more nights per week, it was okay because he was not much of a dancer. She swore on each occasion that she would not be unfaithful to her husband, and she was perfectly serious and focused on her intent to dance and do nothing else. Inevitably, however, she wound up having intercourse, often unprotected, with someone she met in a bar. Afterward, she would feel frightened, depressed, and guilty.

For addicts, the repeated resolution to stop or control their behavior and the failure to do so is not only common but also extremely painful. The failure to control themselves leaves addicts feeling powerless, as indeed they are, and that sense of being out of control is terrifying. Therefore, the addict seeks to avoid this terror by engaging in more of the soothing activity—in this case, sex. Again we see the makings of a vicious cycle. The addict becomes depressed and anxious, partly because of his or her sexual activity, and then needs even more sex to quell the anxiety or deaden the depression.

Increased time spent in activities necessary to obtain sexual activity and/or to recover from its effects.

Ken, like Carrie, the woman whose whole life became sex, spent hours preening himself before going to the singles bars. Because he was compelled to stay until he scored, he was often exhausted the next day when he would obsessively wash his genitals in an attempt to magically escape disease.

Decreased social, occupational, or recreational activities directly related to sexual activity.

I have written elsewhere that at the end of the alcoholic process the drinker is left with an "empty bottle, empty world, and empty self." This is because addictions invade every aspect of life, including mind, body, and spirit, and in this way, lead to progressive impoverishment.

The first manifestations of such impoverishment are emotional and mental. The addict experiences a narrower range of feelings than before, and those feelings that are experienced are often distorted and incredibly intense. The sex addict's emotional life becomes more and more twisted, constricted, and distorted. The addict regresses to using primitive defense mechanisms, the most common of which is denial. Just as the emotional feelings decrease in scope, the addict's mental processes become increasingly narrow and limited. Huge amounts of mental energy go into defending the addiction and finding supplies—into lying, scheming, rationalizing, and defending—so that little mental energy remains for anything else.

The second manifestation of such impoverishment is physical—the body is progressively damaged. This effect is glaring in chemical addicts, although sex addicts may also suffer bodily damage from exposure to diseases—both fatal and nonfatal. Death from medical complications of sexually transmitted diseases affects not only homosexuals but heterosexuals as well.

Finally, there is spiritual impoverishment. One does not have to be religious to be spiritual. Spirituality includes ideas and values that are necessary to mental health. These ideas and values can be quite secular in nature, yet they must in some way provide for transcendence of self. When these ideas and values are lost, spirituality is lost, and life becomes empty. The growing self-hate and self-loathing, the loss of all hope except for the hope to grope, and a numbing bitterness and cynicism combine to form a bleak and negative perspective on life. All of this, accompanied by a loss of faith, leads to ultimate despair. The sexual addict winds up spiritually impoverished, self-hating, and hopeless.

So, you can see, as the sexual addiction progresses, more and more of the addict's life is taken away until nothing remains except the pursuit of sexual activity. Not only was more and more of Tim's time spent preparing for, seeking, and recovering from sexual experiences, but his inner world contracted until, unless compelled by economic necessity, he barely thought about anything else. One by one, his friends dropped out of his life, his interest in books and sports died, and his emotional range became restricted to briefer moments of euphoria after he scored and longer periods of anxiety and depression when he didn't.

Continued sexual activity despite knowledge of persistent or recurrent physical or psychological problems that are caused or exacerbated by the activity.

As previously stated, some sex addicts knowingly engage in their addictive behavior in the face of physical illnesses such as venereal disease or even HIV. Sexual exposure to HIV is sometimes motivated by a self-destructiveness of suicidal proportions. Sometimes it's motivated by such a strong compulsion to have sex that nothing else matters, and in such cases denial ("It can't happen to me") also plays a role. Sex addicts also continue their behavior despite knowing that their activities are causing them psychological distress, including deep shame, guilt, and anxiety. I regularly treat patients who continue their activities in the face of psychological and emotional anguish caused by the internal conflict they feel between pursuing their compulsion and living up to conscious and unconscious expectations of themselves.

Sammy came from an Orthodox Jewish family. He was homosexual, a condition his pious grandfather considered worse than death. Sammy was tormented by conscious guilt about his homosexuality and by unconscious rage he felt toward his family. He had two obsessive thoughts. His first thought was, "Maimonides [a medieval Jewish sage] thought homosexuals should be stoned to death." His second thought was, "Grandfather should shove the Torah up his ass." The only thing that relieved Sammy's guilt and obsessive thoughts was sex. Yet the more sex he engaged in, the more guilt he felt and the more tormenting were his obsessive thoughts, which in turn required more sex to temporarily relieve them— ad infinitum. Sammy was caught in a vicious cycle, and he soon became a sex addict. He then discovered that alcohol also "worked." He reasoned, "At least Maimonides didn't prescribe stoning for drunkenness."

It is important to note that one need not meet all eleven diagnostic criteria to qualify as a sexual addict.

Only three of the eleven symptomatic behaviors need be present for the diagnosis to be made. Diagnostic criteria should not be applied mechanically; rather, the entire context of the behavior(s) and the person's life circumstances should be taken into account. Indeed, there is much danger in taking any of these behaviors in isolation from one another, or even in concert, and labeling them "addiction."

The World Health Organization (WHO), a United Nations agency, has published its own criteria for addiction that I adapt to sexual addiction for diagnostic purposes. First, the behavior must violate community standards; second, the behavior must result in detriment in one major life area, such as vocation, health, or interpersonal relations.

In my practice, I have observed certain characteristics in those whose sexuality appears driven by unconscious demons. The aforementioned 11 criteria amount to symptoms, if you will. I apply additional considerations to these criteria and try to put them into the context of a patient's life, which makes possible a formal diagnosis of sexual addiction. A person's behavior(s) can be considered evidence of sexual addiction if one or more of the following are true:

1. It is compulsive in the sense that the sex addict has little choice but to engage in the sex act or be consumed by the sexual preoccupation regardless of consequences to self or others.

2. It has a driven quality because it is an attempt to fulfill unconscious needs and resolve unconscious conflicts, which, by its very nature, it cannot do. The attempt is futile, and this futility results in meaningless repetition.

3. It is out of control at the behavioral level and engenders conscious or unconscious anxiety at the emotional level because the sex addict "knows" at some level that he or she is out of control.

4. It persists over time.

5. It continues despite damage to health, career, relationships, reputation, or self-esteem.

6. It is at variance with community standards, meaning that it exceeds and goes beyond culturally accepted standards and is damaging to the individual.

7. It progresses in the sense that its negative consequences accelerate and become more serious.

In the following chapters, I will illustrate how President Clinton's behavior meets all these criteria by exploring the patterns that have evolved in his life. How our president finds himself in his current quandary—warding off allegations of sexual impropriety with Monica Lewinsky, Kathleen Willey, Elizabeth Ward Gracen, and even Paula Jones—makes sense and becomes far less perplexing if put in the context of sexual addiction.

Remember: *Sexual addiction is not about sex.* The sexual addict is seeking reassurance, a guarantee of cohesion and continuity of the self; a feeling of being loved, needed, and wanted; and a rise in self-esteem. The problem with using an addiction to fill these voids is that, in the short term, it actually works. Each time a sexual compulsive scores, he or she feels a little more powerful, a little more in control, a little more together, a little more lovable, and a little more worthwhile. If that were the end of the story, it would be a wonderful fix to certain kinds of emotional distress. Unfortunately, that is not the end of the story. In the long run, the fix backfires. The temporary power, control, and feelings of worth give way to an emotional hangover in which guilt, shame, and feelings of powerlessness cause sex addicts to feel even worse about themselves than they did before.

CHAPTER THREE

Planting the Seeds of Addiction

For young Bill Clinton's family, there were serious difficulties even before he was born. Although his family had its strengths, it had its weaknesses as well, and those weaknesses were such that typify dysfunctional families.

The term *dysfunctional family,* like the term *neurotic person,* is redundant. Every family is dysfunctional to some extent, and every family is functional, insofar as it enables its members to survive. Those that we label truly dysfunctional are those in which addiction (or true mental illness) seriously impairs normal parental functioning and results in depravation and/or abuse of the children in that family.

By nature, families are imperfect, just as people are, and children are pretty resilient, so a good deal of what is called *dysfunction* can exist without leaving irreparable scars. However, after a certain point, the problems begin to cause deeply ingrained damage. Families in which there is active addiction, like young Bill Clinton's, are by definition dysfunctional. Addictions so consume those who have them—and so alter their behavior—that terrible things inevitably result. Granted, bad things happen in every family. The difference is, in truly dysfunctional families like Bill Clinton's, they happen chronically and repetitively, predisposing the children in the family to addiction.

Predisposition to addictive behavior occurs as a result of combined biological factors, psychological factors, and societal factors. In other words, addictions have bio-psycho-social determinants. It is these determinants that lay the seeds for addiction.

Our biological makeup is preset by our genes and extremely difficult to change. Just as genes determine your eye color and hair color, they also determine the structure of your brain (or your neurological makeup). Because one's neurological makeup is genetically determined, it is passed, in part, from parent to child. You may wonder, What has this to do with addiction? If you have a certain type of brain chemistry, then certain activities will be more reinforcing for you than for other people. For example, sexual behavior, when addictive, has self-perpetuating, reinforcing qualities. For those with a certain type of brain chemistry, the more they have sex, the more they want to have sex. So, both genetics and neurochemistry go hand-in-hand to predispose a person to addictive behavior.

Our psychological makeup includes temperament; relatively enduring and stable modes of presentation, reaction, and behavior; emotional styles; defensive styles; beliefs and values (perhaps first acquired from others but now our own); ways of dealing with traumatic events; our memories (conscious and unconscious); and our internal (mental) images and representations of ourselves and others (conscious and unconscious). Collectively, these factors constitute a powerful part in our lives and predispose each one of us to a certain lifestyle.

The social factors that determine propensity to addiction include the values, expectations, norms, role definitions, models, and behaviors that we internalize given the environment to which we've been exposed. The family is the first and most powerful environmental influence, but as children mature, the larger society plays a progressively more important role in shaping the way we will be. We are all exceedingly influenced by our peers, and there is a substantial amount of social psychological data to support this notion.

As you will see, all addictions (including sex addiction) are family diseases. This is true in a number of senses. First, addictions are family diseases in that they affect not only the addict but also family members in the addict's life. The addict is closely interlocked with family members who allow the addictive behavior to continue in one of two ways: either by covering up for the addict and making excuses for his or her behavior or by denying (both to themselves and to others) that anything is wrong and ignoring the addict's problem altogether.

Second, addictions are family diseases in that they often cross generations. Frequently, the documentation of an addict's family history will reveal addiction in previous generations. The addictions may not be exact in nature. For example, one generation may have problems with alcohol, and the following generation may have problems with sex; however, the fact is that addictions can and do cross generations. The psychiatrist Murray Bowen, one of the fathers of family therapy, devised an instrument called the *genogram*. The genogram is an intergenerational drawing used to visually demonstrate relationships over three or four generations that affect the current generation. It shows who is related to whom, who married and when, who divorced and when, and who had children and when, who died and when, who had mental illnesses, and who had addictions. It is a useful tool for learning about the impact of the past on the present. For young Bill Clinton, the predisposing bio-psycho-social factors and familial aspects of addiction were present at every turn.

Bill Clinton's mother, Virginia, grew up in Hope, a small town in the southern part of Arkansas. Her father, Eldridge Cassidy, was a small-town ice-delivery driver, and her mother, Edith, worked as a nurse. Eldridge knew everyone in town and was considered a placid, gentle, nice guy. Edith likewise could be gentle, quiet, and loving, but she was also a woman of volatile temper who was subject to outbursts of rage. She sometimes beat Virginia and was also manipulative, controlling, and competitive with her. Needless to say, such parenting had its effects on Virginia. It is quite likely that Virginia learned to act out her anger outside of the home because to do so at home would have been too dangerous. It is also possible that Virginia's relationship with Edith served as a model of behavior that would later keep Virginia in an abusive relationship. Edith was also one with an eye for men and was widely known throughout the town as a "flirt." She wore heavy makeup and raised hell in various ways, all in a time and place where such things were highly unusual. These behaviors also served as models for Virginia.

As young Virginia Cassidy matured, she followed closely in her mother's footsteps, becoming a high-energy, razzmatazz, let-it-all-hang-out kind of woman. She, too, layered her face with makeup, painting on thick, sweeping eyebrows high above their original position. She also dyed her hair black with a bold white racing stripe, smoked two packs of cigarettes a day, drank liquor, and (just like Mom) became an irrepressible flirt.

In 1943, Virginia was living in Shreveport, Louisiana, working as a student-nurse when William Jefferson Blythe brought his girlfriend to the hospital emergency room. For Virginia, it was love at first sight—mad, passionate love. Little did she know that Bill Blythe was quite a character. A traveling salesman with a girl in every town, he had already been married (depending on which biographer you read) four or five times before he met Virginia. Bill Blythe abandoned woman after woman, leaving some of them pregnant or with children. He seemed to run from one scrape to another using various aliases, giving conflicting stories of his birthplace and birth date, and generally leading a life of lies.

Within only two months of their meeting, Virginia, still unaware of Bill Blythe's shady past, married him. Only five weeks later, Bill, an enlisted member of the U.S. Army, was sent overseas, leaving his young wife behind. After his wartime assignment, he returned to the United States and his occupation as a traveling salesman and moved to Chicago. Virginia remained in Hope with her parents while Bill tried to establish a home. After purchasing a house in the Chicago suburbs, Bill headed out across the American heartland to bring back his wife (then pregnant) to finally live with him. He never made it.

Driving crazily, passing other cars at high speed, he lost control and rolled the car when a front tire blew out. Bill Blythe was killed, leaving Virginia a widow and William Jefferson Blythe (who would be born three months later) without a father. The love of Bill and Virginia is a romantic and sad story—passion in the midst of war, secrecy and deception, and little shared time—all suddenly ended in a wild car ride.

William Jefferson Blythe III was born in Hope on August 19, 1946. When he was only one year old, his mother left for a New Orleans school to become a nurse anesthetist. For the most part, young Bill was well cared for by his grandparents, whom he called "Pappaw" and "Mammaw." He was adored by his grandmother and pampered by his grandfather, but mothers are mothers, and in the end there is no substitute. Virginia's desertion had to have had a powerful impact on the infant Bill. In fact, according to one biographer, his earliest memory is of visiting his mother at nursing school and leaving with his grandparents as she was weeping. Such early memories tell us a lot because encapsulated in them are the themes that will be of importance over a lifetime. The theme of Bill's earliest memory is of separation from a woman and deep sadness over that separation. For him, some of this sadness would later turn to anger—anger at his mother for abandoning him when he was just an infant. Bill simply wanted what all children want but can't identify—unconditional love. Because Bill had no control over whether his mother left him, he would later seek control over other women, wanting to possess them in one way or another. This singular event in the young boy's life set him up for a lifetime of endless, unconscious attempts to fill the original emptiness. It was also the first of many events that would lead Bill to problems with trust.

It is easy to see how difficulties with trust come out of such a bad early experience. Eric Erikson, a highly respected psychologist, described eight stages of human growth in which the very first stage is acquiring basic trust. The woman who brings you home from the hospital affects you for the rest of your life, and if you're fortunate enough to have a good nursing experience, not only in terms of nutrition but in terms of warmth, security, bonding, and feeling loved, you will have an optimistic take on life. You will feel sure that the world has good things in store for you, so you will be trusting of both the world and the people in it. Individuals who have difficulty trusting others usually had less than optimal experiences with trust when they were children.

At the age of one, young Bill was without a father, with an absent mother, and being raised by a grandmother and a grandfather. Bill's life with Mammaw and Pappaw appeared fine, but things were far from harmonious in this home, and these first few years were only a prelude to the drama Bill would later face growing up in an alcoholic environment.

Mammaw's continued temper tantrums sometimes took the form of throwing things, smashing things, and berating Pappaw, who, in turn, seemed to live in fear of her. As a result, he was not indifferent to drinking bourbon and branch water to quiet his feelings. Although Pappaw was not an alcoholic, Bill must have learned early on that people used alcohol to anesthetize their feelings. By passively avoiding Mammaw's rage, Pappaw was, in effect, enabling her as a "rageaholic."

Most addicts, including sexual addicts, are helped by *enablers,* sometimes called *co-addicts* or *co-dependents.* Enablers are people who continue in relationships with someone who is actively addicted for compelling, unconscious emotional reasons despite the fact that the relationship is grossly detrimental to the enabler. The role of the enabler is a vital part of the dynamics of addiction. It is very often a mate who enables the addict by making excuses, reinforcing denial, getting the addict out of jams of one sort or another, and doing whatever else is needed to perpetuate the addiction. The enabler may be driven by a wide variety of forces, including guilt, shame, or the unconscious need to reenact the enabler's childhood. It is a lot easier to stay addicted when you have an enabler helping you do it than if you don't. It helps to keep the consequences of your addiction at bay.

We can only wonder how the infant reacted to the sporadic violence in his home. He had to have experienced fear, indeed terror, at witnessing his loving and adoring Mammaw suddenly become a raging lunatic. Whereas Pappaw drank alcohol to avoid the bad feelings, Bill had to develop other ways of coping—ways that would remain with him the rest of his life. At this early stage, he learned how to deny and bury his feelings in order to avoid pain.

When Bill was three years old, his mother, now a nurse anesthetist, returned from her training in New Orleans. Conflicts arose when Mother and Mammaw began to compete for Bill's attention and affection. Mammaw had taken charge of Bill's life while Virginia was away at school, and even though Virginia was now home, Edith saw no reason to relinquish control over her grandson. This set up a highly pathological competition between the two mothers. Perhaps disappointed in what she must have perceived as a weak husband, Edith early found a substitute in her adored Bill, who, in her fantasy, was the strong, heroic male missing from her life. Although Bill sincerely and deeply loved both his mother and grandmother, the endless competition (by both women) for his love and affection enabled him to make that competition pay off. Bill had two overtly sexual women fighting for his attention, and the very circumstances made it all too easy for him to learn an exploitative, manipulative style that would later prove useful.

By the mid-1940s, Pappaw had ended his career delivering ice and had opened a grocery store. One of the hottest commodities sold was bootleg whiskey, and the store became a kind of speakeasy where, at a time when segregation was still the norm, all kinds of characters, both black and white, would hang around, drink, and talk. The store served as a place for Pappaw to hang out and escape his volatile wife. Bill, too, escaped the violent environment, by hanging out with his grandfather. The store was a rich milieu for a budding politician, and Bill learned from an early age how to get along with all sorts of people. He also learned what men did when they got together—they drank.

With Mammaw and Mother around, life in the Cassidy home was extremely sexually charged. Now that Mother had returned home, she continued to model after Mammaw in her flirtatious ways and flashy lifestyle, exposing young Bill to adult sexuality. Although there is no evidence that Bill was the victim of incest or sexual abuse, there was a certain amount of emotional incest that took place in Bill's childhood. Because growing up in a family is intrinsically sensual and sexual, adults can be overseductive without ever touching a child. In addition, the sexual excitement of being favored, adored, and worshipped by both his grandmother and his mother might have overstimulated Bill. It's difficult enough for a well-adjusted individual to distinguish between *love* and *lust* and between *libidinal* and *nurtur-*

ing. If boundaries are blurred beyond normal, such as they were for Bill, then trouble results. Bill's inappropriate early exposure to sexuality taught him to prematurely associate sex with excitement, secrecy, conflict, and intense arousal. Such age-inappropriate feelings may very well have aroused intense anxiety in the boy. Adolescence, which allowed for sexual expression, probably brought relief, and Bill's deep-seated sexual propensities and conflicts went into hiding until they became manifest in adulthood with its very different role expectations. In other words, Bill learned very well how to be an adolescent, but not nearly so well how to be a responsible adult.

Shortly after Virginia returned to Hope, Pappaw introduced her to Roger Clinton. Roger, originally from the neighboring town of Hot Springs, ran the Buick dealership in Hope. He was a flashy guy, somewhat in the mode of Bill's biological father; however, he was not only a ladies' man, sharp dresser, and real high-stepper but also a heavy drinker and gambler who had a history of physically abusing his former wife. Roger was another rageaholic in Bill's life. He was filled with hostility toward women and a strong need to control them. In this regard, as in so many others, a worse role model is hard to imagine.

Bill was four years old when his mother married Roger Clinton in June 1950. By the time he was in first grade, Bill had started calling Roger Clinton "Daddy" despite the fact that Roger never adopted him and rarely paid attention to him. There is something really sad in this—a little boy so desperate for a father that he longs for and runs after a man who ignores him, calling him "Daddy." But there was no Daddy, and the unfulfilled longing remained. It was at this time that Bill Blythe became known as Bill Clinton. Virginia may very well have changed his name because of her need to present the world a picture of a functional, complete family—a family that didn't really exist. She was motivated by both desire and denial.

Now that Virginia had married Roger, his drunken violence did not take long to manifest. Just as Pappaw had enabled Mammaw's violent behavior, Virginia now enabled Roger's. Her enabling may very well have been the result of low self-esteem or because she so desperately wanted to feel loved. Why *should* she leave Roger? After all, her father never left her mother. In fact, if anything, the violence probably felt familiar. It was what she had grown up with and therefore it felt "normal." If she did realize, at some level, that there *was* a problem, she most likely buried the realization in denial.

When Virginia tried to take Bill to visit his dying grandmother in the hospital, Roger refused to let them to go. When she said, "I'll do what I please," he took out a gun and fired a shot over her head. Again, Roger's anger, hostility, and need to control the woman in his life was evident. The police came, and Roger spent the night in jail. Despite this violent episode, Virginia continued her enabling and let Roger return. She, like her father before her, simply wouldn't take action against the violence at home.

Planting the Seeds of Addiction

In the winter of 1952, having sold the Buick dealership in Hope, Roger moved back to Hot Springs, taking Virginia and Bill with him. He went to work for the Hot Springs Buick dealership owned by his far more successful brother Raymond. Roger was aware that Raymond was better at running the car dealerships, and he felt like a failure in comparison. These feelings of inadequacy and failure led Roger to gamble and drink away all the money he made from selling the dealership in Hope. Each time, Raymond would bail him out in a recurrent pattern.

Hot Springs was the worst possible setting in which a womanizing alcoholic and his flirtatious wife could raise a son. It was a wide-open resort town that had once been the headquarters of Al Capone. Its countless whorehouses and gambling establishments ran 24 hours a day. Its officials and politicians were corrupt to the core, yet no one disapproved. Dishonesty was a given— no one was expected to tell the truth. The men of the town were said to have all kept mistresses and to have beaten their wives while maintaining the façade that everything was fine.

Hot Springs also fueled Virginia's previous activities. After accepting a job at a hospital, she continued her drinking and partying. However, she also developed a new interest—gambling. She spent endless hours both at casinos and at racetracks. (Interestingly, gambling addicts are much like sex addicts in that both thrive on the high arousal, the excitement, the risk taking, and beating the odds.) Virginia, like her mother before her, had become a "sensation seeker," living a life that kept her on the edge. Studies about such behavior, pioneered by psychologist Marvin Zuckerman, have shown that certain neurochemical factors predispose individuals to become sensation-seekers. As such, this neurochemistry can be passed from generation to generation, as it was from Edith to Virginia and, as we'll later see, from Virginia to Bill. Based on the lifestyle of Bill's biological father, one could readily argue that William Blythe had a similar sensation-seeking neurochemical composition that was also passed on to Bill.

Once Mom began gambling, she wasn't around much. When she wasn't drinking and gambling at the country club or the racetrack, she hung out at a club called Vapors. Eventually, Roger couldn't stand it, his violent temper escalated, and by the time Bill was six years old, there were accusations and fights almost every night.

Addicts, like Roger, must lie and cover up in order to maintain their addiction; therefore, they know at some level that they, themselves, are not trustworthy. Not wanting to recognize this fault, addicts *project* their distrust onto other people, so they can point to others and call *them* untrustworthy. This kind of projection is the same as criticizing in others the same qualities you dislike most in yourself. The violent arguments in the Clinton home centered around Roger's constant accusations that Virginia was cheating on him. Roger himself was guilty of infidelity, yet instead of acknowledging this distrust of himself, he projected it onto his wife.

Whether or not she was unfaithful, there was always hell to pay at home. Little Bill Clinton must have wanted to do everything possible to shut out the sounds of drunken fits of jealous rage, cursing, screaming, and near violence, but how? How did he cope? He continued to develop more defense mechanisms. Bill had already learned to bury certain feelings because they were too painful; however, he now learned how to cover up and lie to preserve family dignity, to please everyone in an effort to keep things peaceful, to rely on himself and trust no one, and to deny unequivocally that anything was wrong.

Children raised in families with addiction learn early to distort reality—not only to others but to themselves as well. They are caught up in the dilemma of needing to use their wits in every way possible to survive at home in the midst of chaos, inconsistency, and violence. The whole thing is kind of an escalating and self-reinforcing house of cards. Sooner or later it is bound to collapse. At the same time the child learns to survive, he or she is also learning to lie to the outside world or at least to present things in a false way. The child is usually encouraged to do this by the family. This was certainly the case for young Bill.

Respectability was very important to the Clintons, and on the surface they seemed to have it—professional mother, businessman father, shining son—but if anyone were to open the door after eight at night when company wasn't expected, the story would be totally different. To tell the truth about what went on at home would be betrayal, so Bill learned to lie. Dishonesty was already a given in Hot Springs, but for the Clintons, it went one step further. It became *noble*—it preserved the family myth.

Children think that they are responsible for their parents' problems, and as a result they blame themselves. "If the problem is me," reasons the powerless child, "then if only I were a better child, I could make everything perfect." Bill must have believed, "None of this would happen if I were a good little boy. Dad wouldn't be so mean to Mom." As obviously contrary to fact as this is, the attempt to be a good child is a defense mechanism that gives the child some hope. "If it's my fault, then I can have some control." But little Bill didn't have any control, so all he got from such a delusion—both automatic and unconscious—were feelings of guilt, guilt at having been responsible to make things okay and having failed miserably.

Having personally taken on such responsibility, how could Bill not feel shame at the chaos and ugliness in such a home? In addition to the guilt and shame, Bill must have felt rage, too: "Why is this happening to me?" Bill, at a young age, was full of haunting feelings that would never be acknowledged. No one would help the young boy articulate his guilt, shame, and rage.

Alexithymia is the technical term for "the inability to put feelings into words." Alexithymia results when individuals like Bill possess feelings that are so massive, undifferentiated, and gobbled together that the individual is unable to extract any form of sharply characterized feeling. Feelings of great intensity that can't be put into words are often experienced as bodily states. Tension, for example, is a common manifestation of buried feelings, although some hidden feelings may emerge in the form of true physical or mental illness. This is actually a form of regression to an earlier stage of life (such as infancy or toddlerhood) when there were no words available to describe one's feelings. Those who are lucky enough to experience emotionally healthy childhoods learn to label and express their feelings, whereas those from dysfunctional families usually lack this ability.

So, without an outlet for his emotions, Bill's unexpressed feelings were further denied, repressed, and buried. In fact, Bill became an expert at denial.

He didn't deny the fact that his stepfather was alcoholic; rather, he denied the pain that that alcoholism caused. Sigmund Freud described this form of denial as "isolation of affect." This mechanism works by preventing thoughts and feelings from connecting because making the connection is too painful. Those who use isolation of affect as their primary defense tend to be *externalizers*. That is, rather than feeling their feelings and working through their internal conflicts, they reenact them in the external world. Therefore, like Bill, they become the doers, the hustlers, and the aggressors. This defensive style spares its user pain and often results in high levels of achievement. The trouble is, the underlying issues are never really dealt with, so the unresolved, buried, stuffed feelings and conflicts are inevitably expressed in ways that are rarely in the self-interest of the individual. Most commonly, these unconscious conflicts are reenacted, equally unconsciously, in unsatisfactory or self-destructive relationships. They may also be expressed in relationships with addictive activities or substances. Either way, the unconscious reenactment and addiction are the fruits of the isolation of affect and of externalization.

The confusing elements in Bill's life furthered his inability to trust. Everywhere he turned, the outside didn't match the inside, appearances weren't reality, and love was somehow not very loving. Ironically, his mother idolized him and frequently told him how brilliant and wonderful he was and how he could do whatever he wanted. She constantly voiced expressions of her confidence in Bill, instilling extremely high expectations in the young boy, yet she was rarely around. Bill had to have wondered, "Is *this* what love feels like?" Even when mother was home, she was preoccupied fighting with her stupefied husband. Bill knew that Dad loved Mom—after all, they were together—yet Dad was always so angry with Mom and so mean to her. Again, Bill must have questioned, "Is *this* what love looks like?"

Such confusion must have been unimaginable. Who could you trust? Who could you rely on? What was love? What was the truth? Bill desired certainty and predictability because his life was filled with uncertainty and unpredictability. In essence, he sought control. He could control his own achievements, so he set his goals high. When he met them, he felt sure of himself, and he felt powerful.

Now that he had learned to set high expectations for himself, he combined this with his burning desire to please Mom and her constant pressure to succeed. Bill was subsequently set up for perfectionistic striving, and his failure to reach any one goal meant both losing control and letting Mom down, thus plummeting into a pit of pain, shame, and guilt. Failure, therefore, had to be avoided at all costs.

Bill's half-brother, Roger Cassidy Clinton, was born when Bill was nine years old. By the age of 10, Bill was known to be extremely bright and creative, and he continued to present the outward appearance that everything in the Clinton household was just fine. He brought in accolades in an effort to shore up the sagging esteem of the family, and he was always the rescuer. Although mother was intermittently focused on Bill, he still took care of himself and, now, his brother Roger a good deal of the time. He became the missing parental figure both to himself and to his younger brother. Because of this, Roger idolized Bill and often turned to him not only as a father but also as a savior. Those who study alcoholic families have identified a number of roles: "mascot," "clown," "lost child," "hero," and others. These roles are unconsciously adopted by family members as coping mechanisms. Young Bill became the family "hero."

Heroes take responsibility for the family, just as Bill did. Sometimes they literally run the home, doing the domestic tasks normally done by parents, and sometimes they parent the other children. They always fulfill the emotional needs of the adults, becoming substitute husbands or wives to their parents. They also vicariously achieve the unrealized dreams and aspirations of their parents. Although Bill Clinton did not do the domestic chores, he fulfilled all the other responsibilities and duties that should have been met by his mother and stepfather.

Heroes also become overachievers, like Bill, constantly trying to show what good kids they are, believing that their good behavior will "make everything okay." Only then will they feel "safe" and "in control." It is a lifestyle of constant stress because underneath all the accolades and triumphs lies a feeling of emptiness and hollowness— a feeling that something is missing. Because the child never identifies what is missing, as an adult there is an endless quest to achieve more: more power, more money, more women, more whatever in an effort to fill the emptiness. For this reason, addiction has been called the disease of "more." It is a futile attempt to fill a bottomless pit.

One of the most powerful depictions of the hero and the hero's inner emptiness is evident in Orson Wells's classic film *Citizen Kane*. Kane, the film's protagonist, cannot accumulate enough wealth, power, or art. He collects compulsively and is as addicted to power as he is to the accumulation of riches, yet none of his acquisitions bring him any satisfaction. He becomes more and more frantic and desperate, eventually going on a wild, destructive rampage. At the very end of the film he is finally able to tell us (and himself) what it is he has been desperately seeking his entire life: Rosebud. Rosebud was the name of the sled that had been taken away from him when he was a little boy. For Kane, the sled was a symbol of a time in his life when he felt unconditional love and happiness. Sigmund Freud once said, "Great wealth rarely brings happiness because money is not an infantile wish." So true. Addicts do not really want more alcohol, more drugs, more money, or more sex. What they are really seeking is what Citizen Kane sought—unconditional love and happiness.

Heroes, like Bill, can turn dirt into gold, but they pay a terrible price for it. They never get to feel their pain, so they have no choice but to act it out, anesthetize it (with drugs or compulsive activity), or invest a good part of their emotional energy in repressing it. Heroes are always skating on the thinnest of ice over depressive waters deep enough to drown them. They cannot stop—they must keep on skating across that ice, lest they plunge into their despair.

Virginia's continued high expectations for her son only reinforced the hero tendencies in the little Bill Clinton. Inside, Bill was surely filled with pain; outside, he acquired yet one more way of coping. He developed an air of grandiosity and special status—the need to be the very best in order not to feel the very worst. These initial feelings of grandiosity and special status would later combine with Bill's successes in life and lead him to suffer from a condition called *terminal uniqueness*. Terminal uniqueness is a term coined by 12-step recovery programs (such as Alcoholics Anonymous). It refers to an addict's belief that he or she is utterly and completely different from other people, and it's both a blessing and a curse. The blessing comes from feeling unequaled and therefore powerful and special, whereas the curse comes from feeling isolated and lonely. Terminal uniqueness starts as a means of dealing with chronic traumatization: "Unlike other human beings, I'm too special to be hurt by all this." Later the terminal uniqueness serves as a defense of one's addiction: "I'm not like the other addicts—the bad things won't happen to me. I'm too special—too unique." Unfortunately, the reason the uniqueness is terminal is because it inevitably ends in destruction.

As Bill matured into his teenage years, things got progressively uglier in the Clinton home. Roger became overtly violent and began physically beating Virginia. Bill (then 14) stepped in, called the cops, and told Daddy that he would kill him if he tried to hit his mother again. Again, Bill had assumed a parental, protective role toward the entire family, thus living beyond his emotional means.

It doubtless took a great deal of courage for an adolescent boy to take control of the situation; confront an angry, violent man in a drunken rage; and deal with him the way he did. This was the first instance of Bill *turning passive into active*. Turning passive into active is the notion of "doing instead of being done to," and it's a method of coping by mastering your traumatic experiences. By standing up to Roger, Bill was no longer on the receiving end of Daddy's anger; rather, Daddy was on the receiving end of Bill's anger. Bill's action finally gave him a sense of control over life at home.

So, Bill had protected Mom, but he paid a price. As usual, there was no one he could talk to about his feelings, about what happened, and what he had had to do. All his emotions went underground: the shame he felt about his family, the rage at his stepfather and the unfairness of having to be the parent, and perhaps the ambivalent guilt of defeating the father and claiming the mother—really loaded stuff for an adolescent boy. Bill had succeeded in a position he should never have been in. He proved that he could take action, but he had yet to prove that he could deal with his inner emotions.

The violent scenes between Roger and Virginia continued. In 1962, when Bill was 16 years old, Virginia finally divorced Roger—Bill had "won." We can't be sure why Virginia finally divorced Roger, but the decision was certainly triggered by one violent act too many, and she must have been truly afraid by this time. During the divorce proceedings, still wanting to protect his mother and brother, Bill bravely testified in court about the violent and abusive behavior of his stepfather. However, once finalized, the divorce did not last long, and Virginia (over her son's strenuous objections) remarried Roger Clinton that same year. Virginia's remarriage to the abusive alcoholic is another manifestation of her denial, and it made Bill furious. He had finally rescued his mother, confronted a violent grown man, testified against him in court, and risked public exposure of how awful things were at home—of how shameful they were—and now she was taking him back! Bill must have thought, "How can you do this after everything I've done for you? I'll show you what happens when you prefer my stepfather to me!" However, thinking about your anger and expressing it are two different things, and Bill would not release the anger he felt toward his mother. He knew only how to bury painful feelings, and he continued to do so.

Unfortunately, the hidden hostility would later emerge as fuel for Bill's sexually addictive behavior, causing him to pursue women in an effort to dominate and humiliate them (much like he must have wanted to dominate and humiliate his mother).

Despite sporadic attempts to quit drinking, Roger never could stay on the wagon. Although the violence ceased, Roger eventually began to deteriorate as a result of his alcoholism. Alcoholics and other addicts have difficulties taking care of themselves. Once the deterioration starts, it continues to eat away at the addict, and Roger was no exception. By now he was a pathetic figure no longer rousting about town but coming home and sitting depressed and defeated, downing drink after drink. Roger never would clean up his act and become the father figure Bill both wanted and needed.

Let us sum up Bill Clinton's early childhood influences in terms of bio-psycho-social determinants. First, biological influences are found in his maternal grandmother, who was a flirt, a gambler, and a partier and was frequently violent; in his biological father, who was a chronic liar, a womanizer who abandoned wives and children, and a salesman who possessed traits of a con man; and in his mother, who (like his grandmother) was a flirt, a gambler, and a partier. Insofar as proclivities to high-risk, high-energy externalizing lifestyles are built on genetic material, Bill Clinton received this material from both his paternal and his maternal side. Biologically, the seeds of addiction were planted even before Bill was born.

Planting the Seeds of Addiction

The psychological determinants that helped nurture the seeds of addiction included reliance on denial, rationalization, and minimization as primary defense mechanisms; grandiosity and ingratiation (people-pleasing) as an interpersonal style; and perhaps, most saliently, repressed shame, guilt, and rage.

And finally, with regard to the society to which Clinton was exposed, his home environment included the female model behaviors of Mom and Mammaw. The male models included a grandfather who failed to take action against the controlling and violent ways of his wife and a stepfather who was a womanizer, a gambler, and a violent alcoholic. The environment in Hot Springs not only provided models of infidelity in the form of the town's occupants but also was the source of much of the young boy's repression of guilt, shame, pain, and rage. The environment said it was all right to act out but that it wasn't all right to feel. Add to all this the town's whorehouses, racetracks, bars, gambling casinos, and legacy of corruption. If you wanted to design an addictive background, you couldn't top this one. The seeds of addiction were being nourished to perfection.

Bill Clinton's early years were filled with as much exposure to predisposing addictive factors as is possible to have—biologically, psychologically, and socially. The more you learn about Bill Clinton's childhood, the more you realize that he overcame an awful lot, but he didn't overcome the legacy of his early years. The proclivity to addictive behavior lies back in his childhood insecurities, thus the endless need for reassurance that he is lovable, that he is powerful, that he can get what he wants, and that he is accepted. The desire to find such reassurance would not vanish as Bill continued to mature. In fact, not only would it remain a looming presence in his life, but it would feed the addictive behavior that would eventually develop.

Shortly after Clinton's first election to the presidency, I engaged in a debate with Wendy Kaminer, author of the best-seller *I'm Dysfunctional, You're Dysfunctional,* a takeoff on a psychological best-seller of an earlier time, *I'm Okay, You're Okay.* The dispute was over whether the 12-step recovery movement had become the new American religion. Wendy's thesis, elaborated with great wit, is that the 12-step movement has created a generation of crybabies who are given to publicly and exhibitionistically proclaiming their injuries. Although I knew what she was talking about, I didn't agree with her. Somewhere in the course of our debate, Ms. Kaminer cited Bill Clinton as an example of one who grew up in an alcoholic home but who was anything but dysfunctional. She proclaimed him as evidence backing her theory that adult children of alcoholics (ACOAs) were a bunch of crybabies and that one could grow up in such a home and turn out just fine.

Wendy Kaminer was both right and wrong about Bill Clinton. She was correct in seeing the adaptive side of Clinton's response to the traumas of his childhood. He has indeed done well in the way heroes do well, and for that he is to be given full credit. What Wendy missed, however, was seeing the dysfunctional side that set him up for addiction, in his case sexual addiction. On the dust jacket of Ms. Kaminer's book, she admits, with humor, that she is "in denial." Although intended as a joke, ironically, this is the truth. She is in denial of the effects of addiction on children—specifically the effects on the child who became a president.

An Addiction Progresses

BILL CLINTON EMERGED FROM a childhood of conflict, loss, and a strange combination of depravation and overindulgence primed for the development of an addiction. He had, for the most part, raised himself, and by the time he started high school, he had spent a good deal of his childhood alone. Although being alone is not always a negative thing, there are two ways in which one can be alone—there's a healthy way and an unhealthy way.

The great British pediatrician and psychiatrist Donald Winnicott wrote an essay titled "On the Capacity to Be Alone." In this beautiful and succinct piece of writing, Winnicott states that the capacity to be alone (in a healthy way) is a paradox. It seems like it would be the easiest of things, but it's not; rather, it's a human achievement.

Consider a toddler who is raised by a loving parent. As long as the parent is present yet not intrusive (or impinging), that child will slowly internalize the loving parent in such a way that that parent becomes a part of the child. As the child matures and begins to explore the world, he or she will be comfortable being alone because, in essence, the child is not *really* alone—the loving parent is now inside the child and is now a part of the child. On the other hand, if the child is raised with a parent who prematurely abandons him or her, is unable to give the child enough attention, or because of other circumstances is unable to provide the appropriate love and care necessary for healthy development, then the child not only will feel abandoned but also will experience feelings of panic whenever left alone. These feelings of panic when left alone can remain with the child as he or she matures, and, as adults, these individuals may ultimately suffer from the psychiatric disorder called *abandonment depression.*

Feelings of panic when left alone can also predispose children to addiction because addictions are ways (albeit *unhealthy* ways) of being companioned. "I'm not alone, I'm with Chivas Regal." "I'm not alone, I'm with Tijuana Gold." "I'm not alone, I'm with a sex partner."

By the time Bill Clinton reached high school, his life had already been filled with abandonment, and being alone was indeed difficult. Although Clinton had not yet developed a sexually addictive behavior, he had already found one way to avoid being alone—he found high school politics.

A handsome, highly verbal, magnificently articulate, and sometimes glib talker, the adolescent Bill Clinton had developed a charming personality, much like his biological father. Popularity was extremely important to him because he had always desperately wanted to be liked and accepted. He had grown accustomed to pleasing his mother, and now, as he entered high school politics, he became the ultimate people-pleaser. Clinton must have unconsciously believed, "If all these people love me and vote for me, then I have nothing to feel badly about or ashamed of. I must not be such a terrible human being. I must not be responsible for my father's death or my stepfather's drinking, after all." These thoughts echo the underlying, unconscious hopes of every child raised in a dysfunctional home: "The horror at home didn't *really* happen. All these people love me, so the bad stuff can't be real." This is the unconscious message that Bill must have given himself as he ran for school office and, for the most part, won. Clinton was only partly convinced by his own unconscious thoughts, and his doubts about himself remained. However, the denial did help him feel somewhat better about himself, as did the approval and recognition he received from his peers. He quickly rose to leadership positions—academically, politically, and socially.

You may think, as did Shakespeare's Hamlet: If *that's* evidence of pathology, then "Who shall scape whipping?" However, it's not Bill's success that serves as evidence of a problem but rather the forces behind his success. We must examine *why* he was so driven and determined. All human actions are complexly motivated, and it is only by examining the driving forces behind Bill Clinton's accomplishments that we can see how his motives to succeed were unhealthy.

The drive to succeed becomes unhealthy when accomplishments become one's sole source of identity and self-esteem. "I must get an A on this paper, or else I'm worthless." "I must get a promotion, or else I'm nothing." The belief "I *must* accomplish X, Y, and Z, or else my life is meaningless" has been referred to by psychologist Albert Ellis as *musterbation*.

Clinton was so accustomed to playing the "hero," trying to meet both his and his mother's expectations, that he had become a chronic musterbator. His whole identity became wrapped up in his accomplishments. As such, his motivation to succeed was much more driven than the average person's. Failure meant much more than picking himself up, dusting himself off, and trying again; rather, it meant feeling like a "worthless nobody." Meeting goals and being successful, therefore, became a desperate fight for identity, acceptance, admiration, and love. Success meant everything, and because of this, Bill took on high school politics with an intense seriousness that is almost incomprehensible. All of Clinton's biographers have noted that Clinton's friends, without exception, were aware of and impressed by Clinton's serious and intense drivenness during high school campaigns.

During Bill's high school years, his stepfather continued to deteriorate. Bill had given up hope that he could rely on Daddy, so he took it on himself to step into the role of "the father." He made the transition with seeming ease and comfort; however, it was not a healthy role because at the same time he was playing "father," Bill Clinton was also yearning for a father. This must have been incredibly difficult for the adolescent boy, and this initial longing would later become a lifelong search for a man to fill this missing role. Unfortunately, it would also lead Clinton to a series of continuous disappointments as one father figure after another either died, disappointed him, or rejected him.

In some ways, Bill had become not only the "father" of the house but also the "husband" to his flirtatious (and near–sexual exhibitionist) mother. He was now clearly the man in his mother's life. Bill had reconciled himself to the now defeated dying man who sat lonely and drinking as Bill gathered trophy after trophy for his mother to admire. It was during this time that mother turned the home into a shrine, dedicated to the worship of young Bill Clinton. There was something unhealthy in this—excessive and somehow erotic. Virginia must have been terribly desperate for a "man" to love. Through high school, Bill stayed in close contact with his grandmother and remained the darling of both his mother and his Mammaw, for whom he could do no wrong. Bill learned over time that the love of women was not only his due in life but his salvation as well.

By most accounts, Bill Clinton's high school sex life appears to have been pretty normal. There was the girl next door, several Miss Arkansas pageant winners whom he pursued (and perhaps conquered), and numerous other flirtations and dalliances.

In 1965, Clinton left for Georgetown University to study in the School of Foreign Service. He continued to seek admiration and kept up his role as a people-pleaser. Clinton, once again, was the consummate student politician—both running the campaigns of others and running for office himself. His self-esteem continued to be fed solely by his accomplishments. While at Georgetown, his political activities were by far the most emotionally significant in his life. Early on he attracted a coterie of devoted followers who worked hard to advance his cause. His political followers made him feel important, worthwhile, and powerful, and, as before, he was successful, albeit with occasional setbacks.

His political skills were finally honed in his relationships with his professors. In fact, Clinton went out of his way to charm and form a rapport with his instructors, and in the process he often learned what they wanted on examinations. Bill was, in a way, controlling or manipulating his professors to get what he needed from them. His actions were not motivated by vindictiveness but rather by his simple desire to achieve certain goals. Although he gained a solid foundation in political theory, literature, history, and philosophy, some viewed Clinton as the ultimate "brown-nose." Be this as it may, Clinton excelled in the competitive academic environment in terms of both grades and student politics.

In 1966, Clinton spent time working in the Senate office building as an assistant to Senator William Fulbright. It was here that he began to learn the official ways of Washington. These early experiences on Capitol Hill only fueled Clinton's desire to become elected as president of Georgetown's student council. For Clinton, winning the 1967 student council election became the most important thing in the world. He continued to show signs that he needed applause beyond the norm of the political soul. Unfortunately, during that election, Clinton lost support for being too smooth, too glib, and for having held too many offices. It was as if the Georgetown students wanted someone more "real" to represent them, and Bill was upset in more ways than one when he lost the election, sandbagged by a less flashy, less polished opponent. To all outward appearances, Clinton took the defeat fairly well, learned from it, and modified his public presence. However, in private, Bill expressed deep hurt and disappointment to a few close friends, and he became more determined then ever to get elected the next time around.

While in college, Bill continued to see the girl next door back in Arkansas. He also played the field (certainly appropriate for a single college student) and presumably had sex with a number of the women whom he dated.

In November of 1967, Bill's stepfather, Roger Clinton, died from cancer. Bill had returned home to Hot Springs to say his last good-byes, and he was there when his stepfather passed away. Bill was only 21 years old, and he had already lost two fathers. To all outward appearances, Bill had achieved resolution with his stepfather before he died and henceforth presented his late stepfather as an okay guy who had had a problem. His actions were most likely motivated by a combination of both denial and mature compassion.

Even after the death of Roger Clinton, Virginia remained in denial about the effects of his drinking. In fact, she would later write in her autobiography that the impact of Roger's alcoholism didn't bother her at all, even when he would disappear for days.

After his stepfather's death, Bill returned to Georgetown and was excited to learn that he had been chosen as a Rhodes scholar candidate—another great accomplishment to feed his self-esteem. For Bill, his candidacy was made even more of an honor because success at winning the scholarship would mean following in the footsteps of his mentor, William Fulbright, who had been a football star at the University of Arkansas and subsequently went on to become a Rhodes scholar. Clinton, however, had doubts about winning, because most Rhodes scholars were not only high academic achievers but also well-rounded athletes. Although Bill was not much of an athlete, he won the scholarship, balancing out his lack of athletic achievement with his great skill in handling the final interviews. Once again, Clinton was the perfect politician—reading what people wanted and intuiting how to play them. Without any malevolent intentions, he had once more charmed, manipulated, and controlled his way to success.

Clinton's ability to accurately read the feelings and needs of others came from his childhood years in a troubled home. The psychologist Alice Miller has written about this in her famous book, *Prisoners of Childhood*. In it she recounts how roles are reversed in such homes. The children become the "parents" both to their mother and father and to their siblings, hence the term *parentified child* (another name for the hero). These children learn early in life how to read and meet the needs of their parents and siblings. According to Miller, children who play the parental role grow up feeling cheated and deprived, as indeed they are, because they never had any real chance to be a child. As adults, they harbor intense unconscious resentment, which may be left internalized or acted out. If the resentment is not acted out, the internalization leaves the individual vulnerable to depression.

As mentioned before, heroes or parentified children, like Clinton, often become superachievers who do extraordinarily well in academic and vocational pursuits. However, their academic and vocational success comes at the cost of healthy personal relationships. Their ability to be empathic, to be attuned to the feelings of others, allows them to relate to others extremely well; but, on the other hand, these same skills are used in the exploitation of others: "Because I understand you, I can get you to do whatever I want." Such exploitation may not be malevolent or even conscious; rather, it becomes an alternative, unconscious way of getting what one wants.

Clinton's Oxford years certainly broadened him and made him more worldly, and he made friends who stayed with him throughout his career. (It was during this time that he met fellow Rhodes scholar Robert Reich, the man who would later become the secretary of labor during

Clinton's first presidential term.) Clinton's ability to seduce and control allowed him to tame the savage gatekeeper at the university. Although the gatekeeper terrified all the students, he had a fondness for Bill. Clinton did his share of partying at Oxford and no doubt had his share of sex (this *was* the 1960s, after all), but just as in high school, Clinton's sexual behavior was nothing out of the ordinary.

It was during this time that Clinton was exposed to the antiwar movement, and although he was in opposition to the war, he was always careful not to get himself too far out on a limb. He knew from an early age that if he wanted a political career, he could not be labeled a "radical," especially if he wanted a career in a conservative state like Arkansas. Later, Clinton's harsher critics would condemn him for his antiwar sentiments, claiming that Clinton's only interest in avoiding Vietnam was based not on a principled opposition to the war but on an opposition to being shot. Although his relationship with Oxford dons paralleled his relationship with professors at Georgetown, Clinton, anxious to embark on a career in law and politics, left before taking a degree.

Clinton had emerged from his Oxford years with real aplomb. He remained well liked (always one of his paramount goals), had traveled all over Europe, picketed the American embassy in London, and read voraciously. In 1970, he returned to the United States an already polished politician, ready to study law at Yale. From the moment he arrived in New Haven, Clinton was deeply involved in politics—initially behind the scenes. He rarely attended classes at Yale because he was too busy running political campaigns, and it was only a matter of time before he would quit serving as campaign manager and once again become a candidate himself. His extraordinary intelligence allowed him to show up at Yale in time to cram for his courses, take examinations, and then take off again. During those years, he built a network of alliances that would ultimately get him elected to the U.S. presidency.

Clinton's political campaigning set a pattern of intense effort (building toward a climax), followed by disengagement. This sequence of intensity, climax, and disengagement perfectly paralleled the sexual pattern he would later fall into. Bill was a handsome young bachelor interested in lots of young women, and he had his share of relationships with both the girls back in Arkansas and the women he met in New Haven. Then, one day in the cafeteria at Yale, he met a woman different from all the others he had dated; he met Hillary Rodham.

Another academic superstar with political ambitions, Hillary proved to be an attractive challenge to Bill Clinton. She was independent, a quality he admired because his childhood had forced him to become independent. Clinton also respected the fact that she was going to have a career of her own. Although her politics were rather to the left of his, they did not pose any real conflict, and the couple quickly developed a romance. The relationship was far from harmonious, and even from the beginning, it was characterized by public fighting. Although most of the anger seems to have been Hillary's, there were mutual recriminations. It may be said that Clinton was simply engaging in the behavior he considered "normal." Just as Virginia may have equated Mammaw and Pappaw's arguing as part of a "normal" loving relationship, Bill had likewise grown up with arguing between Virginia and Roger, and he may have considered it "normal," too. It may also be said that Bill was finally expressing some of his own repressed anger and hostility during these arguments and may even have been partially identifying with his stepfather's need to control women.

Everyone believed that Hillary Rodham was in love with Bill Clinton, and she probably was. The amount of fighting attributable to his involvement with other women is difficult to measure, but it's reasonable to assume that the affairs constituted part of their difficulties. So, Bill was unfaithful to Hillary from the beginning, and although she protested it, she also accepted it by not leaving him. It appears that he now had someone who loved him, accepted him, and supported him, which is all part of what he sought. So, why did he *still* need other women? At this point, his sexual addiction seems manifest. Hillary was already, in a way, enabling Bill in his sexual behavior simply by not leaving him. Despite their wild and turbulent fights, they ultimately moved in together, and although they were now officially a couple, they were often separated as Bill continued to venture off to engage in various political activities, leaving Hillary behind. It is reasonable to assume that Bill didn't spend many nights alone during his travels.

Bill and Hillary continued to live together during law school. After graduation in 1973, the two remained a couple, but Bill returned to Arkansas to teach law, and Hillary went to Washington to work in various capacities as a lawyer. Clinton, true to form, became popular and successful as a law professor at the University of Arkansas in Fayetteville. Hillary developed an interest in legal issues concerning child welfare and became an early advocate of children's legal rights. While in Washington, Hillary eventually went to work for the House Judiciary Committee, which was then investigating Richard Nixon's Watergate scandal. The committee ultimately recommended that the House impeach Nixon—a recommendation that led to his resignation and disgrace. There is certain irony in Hillary Clinton's role in the investigation and resignation of Richard Nixon, in that later her own husband, as president, would likewise find himself on the receiving end of such an investigation.

In 1974, Bill Clinton took a leave from the university to run for the congressional election. Although he remained in Fayetteville, he regularly commuted to and from Little Rock to work on his campaign. He was informally engaged to Hillary, yet he continued to see other women. Virginia Clinton's obsession with her son had led her in the past to believe that none of his girlfriends were worthy of him (even if they were Miss Arkansas), and she was less than delighted with the average-looking but highly intellectual Hillary. It was at this point that Clinton's sexual activities started to make serious trouble for him. It is important to note that it was *not* that Clinton's sexual behavior had changed but that *the circumstances in his life* had changed. This made what was once appropriate behavior no longer acceptable. Sexual relationships with numerous partners is one thing when one is a young, single college student, but the same sexual relationships are no longer appropriate when one is engaged to be married and embarking on a career as a public official. Although he was supposedly committed to Hillary (who was still in Washington), he had two other girlfriends, neither of whom knew about the other. In effect, he was cheating on Hillary with a girlfriend that he was also cheating on. His relations with women started to attract attention, and, even at this early point in his political career, Clinton's advisors urged him to put a cap on it. He did not.

Clinton's inability to curtail his sexual behavior had now crossed over from his personal to his professional realm. Despite the warnings and recommendations of his political advisors, Clinton found himself unable to control his urges. Even though the potential consequences of his behavior included not only the destruction of his relationship with Hillary but also the destruction of the career he had spent his entire life working toward, Clinton did not, and could not, put a stop to his sexual affairs. His behavior was now officially out of control and characteristic of someone in the throes of an addiction.

Years earlier, Bill had developed a defense mechanism that did not become readily apparent until his own addiction was full blown. Psychologists call it *iden-*

tification with the aggressor. It is the notion of "If you can't beat them, join them," and it is a method of coping that is often used (unconsciously) by children. It simultaneously serves as another way in which addictions become family diseases, passed from one generation to the next.

Identification with the aggressor leads children who have no other way to deal with the horrors at home to tragically repeat the pathology of their parents. It often becomes their only means of survival. I have had countless patients over the years who said to me, "I swore I would never be like that S.O.B. father of mine, but now I find myself beating my kids just like he beat me and drinking just like he drank." Although Bill Clinton did not become an alcoholic like his stepfather, he identified with Daddy by developing an addictive behavior. Whereas Roger used alcohol to avoid dealing with his feelings, Bill used sex, a seemingly perfect choice given his brilliance, charm, and good looks. For Bill, the sex shored up self-esteem and drove away self-doubt. Transferring addictions (from alcohol to sex) may also have made him feel closer to his overtly sexual mother.

Hillary eventually got wind of what was going on in Little Rock and sent her father and brother down from Illinois to work on Clinton's congressional campaign. According to his biographers, friendly and otherwise, everyone in Clinton's circle assumed that Hillary's father and brother were there to spy on Bill and to reign in his sexual proclivities. At this point, Hillary was still fighting the battle that she would later give in to. She would, in fact, spend many years arguing with Bill about his extra-marital sex life and trying to control him while simultaneously and covertly enabling him. Eventually, however, her enabling would be overt. One can only speculate whether the presence of Hillary's family put a crimp in Clinton's style. Even though there were numerous jokes about their function as Hillary's spies, both men were quickly drawn into Clinton's circle and did their best to help his campaign. In the end, though, Clinton lost the congressional election.

Interestingly, the loss failed to bother Clinton for two reasons. First, he was not at all that sure that Congress was the place he wanted to be, so he viewed the congressional election as a rehearsal and remained minimally emotionally invested in the outcome. Second, he felt that he had succeeded—as indeed he had—in making a name for himself and gaining sufficient public recognition. Clinton simply became more determined to run for another public office, so he returned to teaching law at the university and began to prepare for his next political venture.

In late summer of 1974, Hillary left Washington and moved to Arkansas to be with Bill. She knew that living with Bill as an unmarried couple (as they had done in New Haven) would be unacceptable in a Midwest state, so she got her own apartment. In October 1975, they were married, but Bill's extracurricular sex life continued.

One might assume that for Clinton to have married Hillary yet to continue his sexual affairs meant that he lacked a conscience. This is not the case. Although there are addicts who are sociopaths—those who are totally unprincipled and do not have any sort of moral restraints at all—the best evidence we have indicates that this accounts for only 20 percent, at most, of the addict population. Therefore, most addicts do not lack consciences. In fact, it is because they experience guilt for their addictive behavior that they continue to feel badly about themselves, which in turn leads them to further engage in their behavior in an attempt to try to feel good about themselves. So, in effect, addicts continue spinning in the vicious cycle of addiction not because they lack consciences but because they *do* have consciences telling them that their behavior is wrong. In this way, addicts actually become trapped in their addiction by their guilt. Unless they come to terms with the underlying forces beneath their addictions, they have no hope of reorganizing and reclaiming their lives. Clinton had to have known that what he was doing was wrong, but he was caught in a trap that he could not escape.

In 1976, Bill ran for attorney general of Arkansas and won. He and Hillary moved to Little Rock, and from that point on there were continuous rumors about his sex life. The fights between Hillary and Bill continued. It is notable that although Little Rock was not a resort town like Hot Springs (with its history of resident gangsters, gambling casinos, brothels, and so on), it was also not a typical Bible Belt town. It was a worldly, fast-paced place where lots of money changed hands and where casual infidelity by a politician would not cause much notice. In other words, one had to be pretty extreme with regard to sexual behavior to attract the kind of attention that Bill did.

During the late 1970s, Clinton became involved with Gennifer Flowers. According to Flowers, the affair lasted 12 years and apparently was the source of much marital conflict for the Clintons. However, Bill continued to see Flowers despite Hillary's tirades. Clinton's sex life was now a source of public amusement, and Hillary's decision to stay with him was just more evidence of her enabling. When he moved on from attorney general to governor in 1979, the rumors, accusations, and jokes grew exponentially.

During the 1980s, Clinton was in and out of the governor's office. After his first term, he was defeated for re-election (a loss he took rather hard) but then returned for multiple terms. Although publicly extremely amiable and rarely showing anger, those who know him well during his pre–White House years reported that outbursts of rage and temper tantrums were not uncommon on the part of the governor. These outbursts were partly an unconscious identification with his stepfather, who had ranted and raved when drunk. These episodes were also partly unconscious displacements of the rage that Bill had felt as a child but could not express and suggest feelings of entitlement—"the world owes me because of the bad time I had as a kid." When the world was not giving him what he felt he was entitled to, when people were not jumping fast enough, Bill responded with rage.

His extramarital sex life (and tales about it) continued throughout these years, unstopped even by the birth of his daughter, Chelsea Victoria, on February 27, 1980. (Although Chelsea's birth did nothing to curtail his extramarital affairs, Bill reportedly is an extremely loving parent, perhaps in part as a result of a self-made promise to be a better father than the one he grew up with.) Between 1983 and 1985, Clinton allegedly used Arkansas State Troopers (serving as personal security to the Clintons) to bring women to him. In essence, it was said that he was using the State Troopers as his "suppliers." Clinton would spot a woman he wanted and, in an incredibly dehumanizing way, would send a bodyguard to bring her to him. It was at this point that Clinton began trying to control women by objectifying them. He ordered women to be brought to him as if they were objects, or items on a menu, rather than actual human beings. Clinton did not attempt to establish any type of a relationship with these women, nor did he even engage in the niceties of seduction. Rather, he chose to further degrade them by simply exposing himself and asking for oral sex. Interestingly, Clinton's preference for oral sex is related to more than just the sexual pleasure that such an act brings. Having a woman perform fellatio puts him in a position of power and dominance and gives him the illusion of controlling the woman.

Again, Clinton's inability to control his sexual impulses is the only rationalization that would account for such blatant disregard of the potential personal and political consequences of such sexual behavior. His behavior was so far out of control that he was unable to stop himself from going after the women he wanted to possess. Clinton's use of the State Troopers to procure women unnecessarily exposed him not only to the risks of public disclosure and political damage but also to the risk of blackmail. Despite this, Clinton apparently lacked any concern that the Troopers would take action against him. His continued feelings of grandiosity and entitlement, as fed by his success and power in the political world, made Clinton believe that he was beyond reproach.

Clinton had indeed become like most addicts, tending to ignore the usual social restraints and norms to maintain their addiction. All addicts believe that they themselves are above the rules that govern everyone else, and because of this belief, such individuals are prone to lying and justifying their actions with self-righteous rationalizations. Whether or not one suffers from such a delusion may be easily determined by the administration of a widely used psychological test called the Minnesota Multiphasic Personality Inventory (MMPI). The MMPI measures what is called the *psychopathic deviant scale* (also called the "angry scale") to determine whether individuals are mildly antisocial, believing that the rules don't apply to them. Ironically, all of Clinton's feelings of entitlement and grandiosity had originated during his childhood as compensation for their polar opposites—feelings of self-hatred and self-loathing.

Early in Clinton's life, his feelings of grandiosity, entitlement, and terminal uniqueness had served as coping mechanisms—a form of self-glorification that helped him fight his underlying self-doubt. As Clinton matured, his grandiosity, entitlement, and terminal uniqueness continued to reassure him of his worth and his greatness: "People love me! I can do anything!" What Clinton did not seem to realize is that even popular, well-loved politicians can be devastatingly lonely. As a corollary to Winnicott's idea that "being alone is easier if you've internalized love from your parents," it is also possible for one to be surrounded by people yet feel utterly lonely. Simply stated, just because you are surrounded by people (whether they be friends, family members, political supporters, or heads of state), unless you connect with them on a personal level, you can still feel completely alone. Try as he might, the kind of emptiness that Clinton carried with him from his childhood could not be filled by the adoration of his political supporters or by the sexual encounters with countless women.

Now that Clinton's sexual behavior had become addictive, the same feelings that assured him of his self-worth would serve to justify his sexual behavior. In fact, all sex addicts tend to believe that "the rules don't apply to me, I'm above it all, and I am entitled to do whatever I damn well please."

It is important to note that Clinton's sexually addictive behavior was (and continues to be) partially driven by an unconscious compulsion to recapture the mother who initially abandoned him and who was later simultaneously overinvolved and underinvolved with him. Just like Citizen Kane's endless quest for "more wealth," Clinton's quest for "more sex" had become unconsciously motivated by the delusional belief that "this time, I'll feel just as special and just as wonderful as when I was adored and worshipped as a child." However, despite Bill's attempts to reconnect with his mother, no woman would ever be able to fill the emptiness left by early traumatic experiences, so the search would continue. One woman would follow another, but the emptiness would remain. According to the disgruntled State Troopers, by the mid-1980s, Hillary and Bill had become extremely vindictive and malevolent during their frequent arguments.

The Clintons became heavily involved with church activities during this time. According to one biographer, Bill Clinton was not seeking repentance but rather acceptance, not judgment but rather unconditional love.

It was also during this time that Roger Clinton, now in his late 20s, got into serious trouble. Despite his childhood admiration for his big brother, Roger had not excelled like Bill either scholastically or vocationally. Lacking Bill's strength, brilliance, and drive, Roger instead had stumbled from failure to failure, much like his father. In 1984, Roger was arrested for dealing cocaine. Clinton also learned that Roger not only had been selling the drug but had developed an addiction to it as well.

It was not an accident that both Roger and Bill wound up addicted—one to cocaine and the other to sex. The childhood environment predisposed both sons to addiction and high-risk behaviors. Additionally, both sons had developed feelings of grandiosity—each believing himself to be "untouchable." It is of interest to note that the relationship between Bill Clinton and his younger brother now paralleled that of Raymond Clinton (their uncle) and Roger Clinton (their father). Raymond and Bill were both the successful, older brothers, and they both had younger, less successful brothers who developed addictions.

One wonders what Bill felt when he learned of Roger's addiction and arrest. In his own mind, he probably viewed the incident as evidence that he had essentially failed as a "parent" to Roger, though he did not enable Roger's behavior. Following the arrest, Bill had some brief therapy with an addictions counselor. However, he apparently never regarded himself as the patient but rather believed he was simply being supportive of his brother's recovery. Bill was again acting as a parental figure toward Roger. Still, Bill must have gained some insight into the dynamics of addiction because he bought numerous popular books on adult children of alcoholics (ACOAs) and on alcoholic families. For a period of several months, he appeared fascinated with this newfound information, and he even commented to friends and associates that, until that time, he had never realized how much he had been affected by his stepfather's alcoholism. However, Bill never realized that he was using sex the same way his stepfather had used alcohol and his younger brother had used cocaine, and, unfortunately, he didn't stay in therapy nearly long enough to "work through" his own problems.

Freud's notion of "working through" states that an individual can't deal with lifelong problems and issues in just a few moments of genuine insight; rather, one must revisit the same painful traumatic events and their effects many times before being released from their power. Working through is really work. You have to stick to it and put a great deal of effort into it, and there is no evidence that Bill Clinton did that, although he gained some intellectual insight into the fact that he was an ACOA (and carrying emotional baggage characteristic of ACOAs).

The fact that Bill didn't use this information to help recognize his own need for recovery isn't necessarily surprising. All addicts suffer from a condition called *emotional arrest*. Emotional arrest is the inability to emotionally mature, and it occurs naturally as addictions progress and take over all aspects of the addict's life. You simply cannot grow behind an addiction.

Ironically, Bill made an interesting comment during this time. He stated something to the effect that everyone has an addiction to power, gambling, sex, or something else. His statement was true enough, but he seems to have missed the point—that he, himself, had an addiction. In speaking generally and philosophically about the human condition, Clinton unwittingly copped to his own problem. Lacking the realization that he needed help, Clinton had no choice but to continue his sexually addictive behavior.

In 1987, as Clinton geared up for the 1988 presidential election, one of his oldest and strongest political associates, Betsey Wright, quietly compiled a list of his extramarital involvements. She and others close to Clinton were concerned that on the heel of the Gary Hart–Donna

Rice scandal, it was possible that revelations about Clinton's infidelities would likewise damage his campaign. The people who were most invested in Clinton's political career and his advancement to the presidency were deeply worried that his "zipper problem" would lead to disaster. In fact, Wright was so concerned with the implications of the list that she discouraged Clinton from running for the presidency. Wright and her associates were not trying to hurt Clinton—they were simply trying to protect his vulnerability, and he *was* vulnerable. Their plan was to prepare for attacks on Clinton's character (secondary to his sexual adventures) by having a list of the women with whom Clinton had been involved and pre-cut responses to the accusations, regardless of what they might be. The roster was jokingly referred to as the "doomsday list." It was said that Clinton had been with so many women that not only could he not remember their names, he had no idea how *many* there had been.

The "doomsday list" compiled by Clinton's supporters serves as crystal-clear evidence that, during his last term as governor, Clinton's sexually addictive behavior had not stopped. The behavior had become more impulsive, compulsive, and all-consuming, and it clearly rode over his better judgment time and time again.

The relationship between impulsiveness and compulsiveness has baffled generations of psychiatric and psychological theorists. Addictions are strange in that they are both impulsive *and* compulsive. Addicts are extremely impulsive in the sense that they need their fix (be it drugs, alcohol, or sex), and they need it *now*. Addicts are also compulsive in that the delay of gratification feels impossible, so the addict is driven—or compelled—to impulsively engage in more addictive behavior. In other words, addicts, like Clinton, are compelled to be impulsive.

In May 1991, Clinton attended a conference at the Excelsior Hotel in Little Rock. While there, he met Paula Corbin, who was working as a secretary for the Arkansas Industrial Development Commission, the organization that was sponsoring the conference. Despite past warnings by political advisors, the compilation of the doomsday list, and the knowledge that he was currently campaigning for the U.S. presidency, Clinton again used State Troopers and had Paula brought to his hotel room. Clinton's actions at this time were nothing but foolish, reckless, indiscrete, and characteristic of a man who had lost control of his actions. Clinton, in continuing to use State Troopers to further his sex life, again unnecessarily risked public disclosure and political damage. He still continued to believe that the rules no longer applied to him—he was special, entitled, omniscient, and omnipotent.

The Gennifer Flowers story broke in 1992, during the general election. Clinton initially denied having had the affair but later partially admitted to it. The important thing to note is that Clinton now knew that his sexual conduct would be under relentless media scrutiny, but this knowledge did nothing to stop his behavior. His inability to curtail his affairs, given this information, was indeed evidence of an addiction.

An Addiction Progresses

By the time the Clintons left Arkansas for Washington in 1992, Bill was notorious in Little Rock for his sexual escapades. His continued sexual behavior even after winning the presidency and taking up residence in the White House illustrates exactly how futile the musterbator's external accomplishments were when it came to bringing contentment. Just like Citizen Kane, Clinton's great achievements and acquisitions could not compensate for the love lost in childhood.

In October 1993, Clinton's 1985 gubernatorial campaign was named by the Resolution Trust Corporation (RTC) investigator Jean Lewis as one of nine criminal referrals made as a result of her investigation into the dealings of Madison Guaranty Savings and Loan—the Whitewater issue was officially in the press and under investigation. Clinton again knew that, from this point on, his actions would be carefully scrutinized, but his sexual escapades continued.

On November 29, 1993, Kathleen Willey reportedly became an unwilling participant in Bill Clinton's sexual acting out. She had long been a Clinton supporter and enthusiast, had helped him in his political campaigns, and at the time was working for him gratis at the White House. She approached Clinton in a small room just off the Oval Office and told him that she was distraught because of a family situation (a situation that tragically led, later that night, to her husband's suicide). She asked Clinton if he could help her get a paid job because she was no longer in a financial position to work as a volunteer. In the absence of an addiction, what happened next would be truly incomprehensible.

During her conversation with Clinton, not only did he fail to help her in her crisis, but according to Willey, he also grabbed her, groped her breasts, and placed her hand on his penis. Clinton's total lack of consideration for this distraught woman is almost inconceivable, and the irrationality of his actions are readily apparent when one considers that Clinton knew full well about the investigation into his 1985 gubernatorial campaign. He *must* have known that those who wanted to see him fall were scrutinizing his every move. Nevertheless, he risked getting caught making sexual advances, in the White House, with both Secret Service agents and White House staff members close by.

Not only was the time and location risky, but unless Clinton assumed that Willey's political support meant that she would not mind being personally abused, he had no reason to believe that she would keep her mouth shut. To assume that Willey did not mind being personally abused would be a ludicrous assumption and one necessarily driven by grandiosity, entitlement, and terminal uniqueness. Willey reportedly confronted Clinton, asking, "Aren't you afraid of discovery?" Yet he simply brushed it off as if there was no chance he would ever get caught. Not only was Clinton not worried about being discovered, but the potential for getting caught had partially motivated his actions. Feelings of grandiosity and entitlement were initially present when Clinton fondled Willey, and his ability to engage in such behavior under high-risk circumstances further affirmed his feelings of grandiosity and entitlement. He was certain that he could do anything *and* get away with it.

To try to seduce someone who is emotionally upset and looking for support is an old story—not a very admirable one, certainly, but common enough. But to grope, fondle, and physically accost someone looking for compassion and help is over the line. No one has suggested that Kathleen Willey intimated or acted in any kind of way to invite being treated in such a manner. The most reasonable explanation of what happened is that Clinton's actions once again were simply beyond his control. All considerations of prudence, decency, and compassion flew out the window.

This is not, however, to say that Clinton is a sociopath—he does have a conscience, and he has repeatedly shown himself to be a man of considerable emotional depth, capable of compassion and empathy. He also does not appear to enjoy being cruel. Because of this, his actions are best explained in light of an addiction.

Recovering addicts often tell of the deep shame they feel about the things they once did to get their drug of choice. They commonly recount the loss of moral values while they were in the throes of their addiction. I know of one addict who was so desperate for money to buy drugs that he took his grandmother's colostomy bags in the hope of selling them. Once he was in recovery for his addiction, he could not believe that he had done such a thing. Such stories are legion and common.

I am not suggesting that sex is immoral in any way, though taking advantage of a person in Willey's emotional state is. Clinton's actions with Willey are not illustrative of either an amoral or a rotten person. Rather, such actions are a violation of the man's own values and are entirely consistent with one in the grip of an addiction.

Clinton's aggressive actions with Willey also suggest an unconscious enactment of the buried rage left from Clinton's childhood. Clinton undoubtedly rationalized, "She is saying 'no,' but she means 'yes.' I just need to persuade her a little more." Behind this aggression is the desire to dominate and humiliate, again just as Clinton must have wanted to dominate and humiliate Mother after she remarried Roger.

January 1994 brought the Paula Corbin Jones story into the media, when David Brock reported in *The American Spectator* that Clinton used the Arkansas State Troopers to procure women, including a woman named "Paula." Paula, herself, came forward in February 1994, saying that she was the "Paula" whom troopers had brought to Clinton. Clinton's private behavior was more public than ever, but it didn't stop him from going after other women.

As previously mentioned (see Chapter One), Clinton's involvement with Monica Lewinsky occurred during the period in which Clinton lost three very important figures in his life. Clinton's mother died on January 6, 1994; Israeli Prime Minister Yitzhak Rabin was assassinated on November 4, 1995; and U.S. Commerce Secretary Ron Brown was killed in a plane crash on April 3, 1996. Although greatly affected by those losses, Clinton was unable to mourn them completely because his duties as president forced him back to work. He had lived his entire life burying painful feelings, and he did it again as a way to cope with his losses and to move on.

Addicts are addicts because they need to avoid certain feelings and addictions are anesthetics. However, just because someone has an addiction does not necessarily mean that that person is emotionally repressed or suppressed across the board. It is the *particular* emotions connected with the traumas of childhood, and with the addiction itself, that are most frequently anesthetized, acted out, diverted from, avoided, or reenacted in the addiction. The result is a split within the addict between the part that is capable of a full range of emotional response and the part that is not in contact with painful feelings. Bill Clinton possesses such a split. At times he has exhibited a full range of emotional capacity, expressing joy, anger, sorrow, grief, compassion, sympathy, and empathy. At first glance, this sounds like the description of a pretty healthy person.

Fritz Pearls, the psychiatrist who developed Gestalt therapy, a form of therapy that puts a premium on emotional expression, said that the healthy person is characterized by the ability to experience "joy, anger, grief and orgasm." There does not seem to be much question that the president is capable of experiencing orgasm, and I think we would have to concede that he has the capacity for joy, anger, and grief. So where is the problem? The problem is in the selectivity of emotions that Clinton is able to express and respond to.

Although he has recognized himself as an ACOA, he has not relived or worked through his deeply buried emotions from years spent in an alcoholic home. His capacity for grief is also questionable. One may be capable of mourning and yet not mourn a particular loss—the loss of his real father, the loss of his mother, even the premature loss of his own childhood.

Just like the Jones and Willey encounters, Clinton's sexual advances toward Lewinsky were not the actions of a rational thinking, fully collected and composed man. Clinton knew that Whitewater investigators (now including Special Prosecutor Kenneth Starr) were keeping an eye on him; yet once again, Clinton risked engaging in such behavior while in a room at the White House, and once again Clinton had failed to control his sexual impulses. No man in his right mind would risk the presidency and everything he had worked so hard for to engage in a meaningless sexual encounter—unless he was caught up in a sexual addiction.

The one common denominator that makes Clinton's behavior appear addictive is his inability to keep his private life private. This was problematic for Clinton even before his actions were under the kind of scrutiny that has been brought about by the Whitewater investigation.

Indeed, his recklessness and indiscretion simply do not make sense unless Clinton is viewed as a sex addict.

In addition to the cases that have received wide publicity (Flowers, Jones, Willey, and Lewinsky), allegations of sexual encounters with women, most of whom who were apparently willing, have trailed Clinton throughout his career. There are at least a dozen others who have been named in the press and elsewhere, some of whom have maintained that they were involved with Clinton and some of whom have denied it. Clinton himself has remained in denial over all these allegations. He has reinstituted his childhood defense mechanism, although he's no longer covering up Daddy's addiction—he's covering up his own.

Whereas distorting reality was once a necessity to cover up the ugliness in Clinton's childhood home, it is now a necessity to cover up the ugliness in Clinton's adult home. President Clinton has denied all of the sexual charges. Not only has he denied them, but his attorney, Robert Bennett, has stated that he has never seen the president so angry and upset. Bill Clinton has automatically and unconsciously revised reality to defend his addiction. He is perfectly sincere when he becomes outraged at Willey's account of what happened because in his mind he is innocent. Denial, repression, and distortion are standard defenses of addicts, and all of these are standard defenses from Clinton's childhood.

Clinton's compulsive need to have one woman after another continues to be an attempt to reconnect with his mother and to have a more satisfactory relationship with her than he had as a child. However, no other woman can replace Mom, so the search goes on. The only way to break the cycle is to recognize the real need—the need to mourn the separation and loss, not only of his mother's death but of her abandonment when Bill was an infant.

In addition to wanting a more satisfactory relationship with Mom, much of Clinton's sexual activity can be seen and understood as an endlessly repeated attempt to recapture the feeling of being adored—indeed worshipped—by women. Each conquest was an attempt to recapture an illusionary paradise and to create one that had never existed at the same time. He searched for Paradise Lost and yet, at the same time, knew deep down that he never had a paradise at all.

Part of the problem with using sex to recapture lost love and adoration lies in the fact that relationships in sexual addiction are pseudorelationships. These pseudorelationships serve as ways of *seeming* intimate without actually *being* intimate. There is a meeting of physical body parts, but not of the mind or the soul. This is by necessity because sex addicts have difficulties with intimacy. The sexual contacts—often brief and with people with whom there is little connection—are a kind of pseudointimacy. Notice the paradox here. On the one hand, sex, being the most intimate of acts, can be a way of achieving ultimate closeness to another person. On the other hand, however, it can be utterly impersonal. Clinton's sexual encounters illustrate this parody of intimacy. Clinton engages in highly intimate encounters with women yet reveals little or nothing of his self in the process. In fact, he does not even appear to care about the other person's feelings at all. Time and time again, Clinton has shown total disregard for the women as people and has treated them as objects.

Closely connected to the notion of intimacy is trust. To truly commit yourself to another person in an open and deeply intimate way requires a strong capacity for trust. You have to be able to make yourself vulnerable to the other person. Although all human beings naturally have some difficulty completely trusting others, addicts, relatively speaking, have an incredibly difficult time trusting anyone at all. Because Clinton was abandoned numerous times and in numerous ways throughout his life, he never had a reason to trust anyone except himself.

Trust never becomes a necessary element of sex addicts' pseudorelationships because the sexual encounters are too brief and fleeting. In fact, the short-lived nature of sexual experiences such as Clinton's do not give sexual partner a chance to be untrustworthy or to betray the addict.

Individuals with addictive behaviors, such as Clinton, also have difficulty allowing themselves to depend on others. Again, Clinton's early years speak for themselves, and I have already illustrated how his childhood was filled with events and circumstances that made him believe that he could not depend on anyone except himself. This inability to depend on others followed Clinton into his adult life, and when he became trapped in a dependency conflict that would help spin the vicious circle of his addiction.

The dependency conflict theory states that alcoholics depend on alcohol because they are too afraid to depend on other people. Developed by William and Arline McCord, a husband-and-wife research team, the theory was elucidated it in their book *The Origins of Alcoholism.* The basic idea is that alcoholics never admit that they need anyone or anything else at all, thus denying their dependency needs. The alcoholic's inability to admit to needing other people is called *counterdependency.* As the addiction progresses, the dependency on the booze becomes more and more glaring until finally the alcoholic becomes so ill that he or she collapses and has to be "nursed." Now the addict is literally dependent in an infantile way, and things have come full circle.

A similar notion exists with the sex addict. The addict acts as if he or she did not really need anyone except as a receptacle. Sex addicts deny their dependency needs even though they are dependent on "scoring" to maintain their already low and fragile sense of self-worth: "I don't need people, I just need to have sex," is the underlying belief.

There is a part of Clinton that is apparently capable of acknowledging, at a deep emotional level, his dependency needs and of satisfying them in healthy ways, as evidenced by friendships with Ron Brown and Robert Reich. However, there is also a part of him that is far more needy than he cares to admit. Clinton tries to meet these deeper and more unconscious dependency needs by adding notches to his belt.

Although the number of sexual partners does say something about the strength of a sex addict's compulsion, it is not the sheer quantity that determines whether addiction is present. Rather, sexual addiction is better evidenced by the compulsiveness of the behavior and the loss of control in the search for new partners. In fact, Betsey Wright's laundry list brings to mind Leoporello's "catalogue song" in Mozart's opera *Don Giovanni.*

Leoporello, the Don's long suffering servant, tells of his master's conquests (much like Wright spoke of Clinton's conquests): *"In Italia seicento e quaranta,/ in Alemagna duecento e trentuna,/ cento in Francia, in Turchia novantuna,/ ma in Ispagna son già mille e tre!"* "In Italy six hundred and forty,/ in Germany two hundred and thirty-one,/ a hundred in France,/ ninety-one in Turkey,/ but in Spain there are already one thousand and three!" A Clintonian catalogue song would be a sure-fire hit: "In Arkansas . . . ,/ in D.C. . . . ,/ in Virginia . . ."

Having said all this, it still is the case that President Clinton himself has precipitated the present crisis. He easily could have avoided the Monica Lewinsky debacle but could not do so for compelling emotional reasons, namely, because he was in the grip of the stringent necessity of denying and protecting his addiction.

For Clinton not to have settled with Paula Jones was madness. None of the Monica Lewinsky and related matters would likely have come to the public's notice if the Jones suit had not gone to the discovery (examination-before-trial) stage. Robert Bennett, Clinton's lawyer in the Jones case, has repeatedly stated publicly that early in the suit Clinton could have settled for relatively little money and not much in the way of a public apology and that later in the suit he could have settled for more money but did not do so because, as Bennett stated, "The President isn't going to admit to something that he didn't do."

If Clinton genuinely did not do anything inappropriate with Jones, his reluctance to settle would be understandable but still foolish. Knowing that much more information inevitably would have come out at the Jones trial, why not throw some money at her and get rid of her? Clinton could not do this because it would entail more or less admitting to himself that his sex life had been out of control.

The denial that is so characteristic of all addictions would not allow Clinton to admit to his sex life being out of control. Denial is considered pathognomic of addiction; that is, denial is so much a hallmark of such addiction that it pretty well serves to diagnose that addiction. Denial lies at the very heart of every addiction. Let us assume that whatever went on in that hotel room with Jones could be interpreted in different ways, depending on the eye of the beholder. Clinton, in order to affirm his perception of the incident, would had to have seen it in a way that distorted reality. Therefore, he could not have allowed himself to admit, even to himself, that his behavior on that occasion could have been reasonably construed differently by a woman—a low-level state employee—in the presence of a powerful governor.

Jones's motives, however nefarious, are irrelevant to my argument. Even if Clinton and his attorneys are correct in thinking that she is a tool of Clinton's most unsavory political opponents or that she is a gold digger totally lacking in principal, it makes no difference. Not settling was still reckless and stupid and any other explanation of his not negotiating the settlement seems untenable.

You may say, the president was merely following legal advice. Perhaps he was, but lawyers can advise only on the basis of what they understand to be the truth. If Clinton is lying to his attorneys or deceiving himself as to the meaning of his actions, there is no way his attorneys could have given him sound advice. And certainly, in the final analysis, Clinton himself made the final decision, whatever advice he may have been given.

Alan Dershowitz, the brilliant Harvard professor who achieved notoriety as part of the O. J. Simpson defense team, stated long ago on *Geraldo Rivera Live* that Clinton's attorneys were advising him extremely poorly when they did not urge the quickest, and therefore least damaging, settlement with Jones. Unquestionably, time has proven Dershowitz correct. But, you say, Clinton expected to win before the Supreme Court, and neither he nor his attorneys anticipated that the Court would allow the suit to go forward during his presidency. Well, that much is probably true, but after the Court decided against Clinton, the suit was still not settled. Jones seems to have been motivated mainly by greed, and it likely was possible to throw some money her way and get rid of her before the avalanche of totally predictable disclosures swamped the Clinton presidency. Clinton's actions reek of a blindness to consequences that seems uncharacteristic of his general caution and brilliance—a blindness caused by irrationality, compulsiveness, and an addiction.

CHAPTER FIVE

The Master Seducer

CLINTON HAS BEEN LOVED "not wisely but too well," and the legacy of that love was to both shape the master politician and plant the seeds of the master politician's self-endangerment. Given Clinton's childhood conflicts and the stormy and unreliable nature of his home life, his early interest in and choice of politics as a career is not surprising. What better way to avoid feeling alone and to feel constantly supported, needed, and admired than becoming involved in politics? Although Clinton never lacked attention at home, the kind he received was not necessarily the kind he needed. Being simultaneously idolized and not loved for his "real" self (the self that was wounded, hurt, angry, and shamed), the young Bill learned early to addictively look for love in the form of approval from crowds and supporters.

Ironically, the love he compulsively sought in the public realm had exactly the same flaws as the love he received at home and needed so desperately to supplement. He developed friends and followers during even the earliest of his political ventures and used them to meet unrecognized emotional needs. Clinton sought love and acceptance not only at home (as every child does) but also from his classmates, his first constituents, and later from all and sundry. The support, admiration, attention, and love that Clinton needed were *unconditional* and operated on two levels. On the conscious level Clinton sought unqualified adoration from others, and on the unconscious level he sought love and acceptance of the "real" Clinton, the hurt, angry Clinton child whom he had buried. Unfortunately, the love he actually received from his political supporters was the polar opposite of unconditional.

Public adoration for political figures always has been, and always will be, completely *conditional*. Clinton knows that if he does not please his followers, they will abandon him. It takes emotional security to risk loss of love for the sake of principle, and because Clinton lacks the inner certainty necessary to risk the loss of love, he has learned to protect himself from emotional devastation by walking the fence. In the process of keeping everyone happy, of making sure that everyone likes him, he has lost conviction and, politically speaking, come to stand for very little. In this way, Clinton's addictive personality—his out-of-control need for acceptance, admiration, and unconditional love and support—affects him as a leader, which in turn affects our country and each and every one of us.

To understand the dynamics of Clinton the person and how his childhood years have affected his political years, it is helpful to examine the work of the late Heinz Kohut, a great psychiatrist and psychoanalyst. Kohut began his career as a classical analyst but, well into midlife, realized that the Freudian take on things no longer adequately accounted for his patients' problems or his relationships with them. He began to realize that certain patients related to him as if he were not a separate person, and they did this in either of two ways. Either they put him on a pedestal and idealized him, seeing him as the source of all strength, wisdom, and power, or they did the opposite and unrealistically saw themselves as a source of all strength, wisdom, and power.

Kohut called the first way of relating *idealizing* and the second way *mirroring*. In the first case, his patients idealized him by putting him on a pedestal; however, they did so to control him, so they gave him all that power, wisdom, and glory, but it was in their service. In the second case, the patients wanted him to mirror, or reflect back to them, how wonderful and great they were. In either case, Kohut realized that he was not important in himself but only as a screen for the patient's projections or as someone to mirror back to the patient what the patient wanted to hear.

Kohut realized that what he saw was not simply the sickness of patients in psychoanalysis but also a revelation of something important about all human beings and how we work. He developed a theory that used his experience with adults to give a general account of human development. Kohut concluded that, as infants, we are in a state of confusion—a state that the great American psychologist William James called a "booming, buzzing confusion." At this stage, there is no developed sense of "self" but simply experiences of pain and pleasure. Kohut's label for this stage was the *fragmented self*. If individuals become stuck in the stage of the fragmented self (or revisit it either in the course of a psychiatric illness or while under extreme stress), they are, by definition, psychotic because they are in too many pieces—they are too fragmented—to make sense of either the world or themselves.

Of more interest for our purposes is Kohut's second stage, which develops around the age of two and is fully realized when the child has acquired the use of language. In this stage, the pieces come together, and the child develops a sense of continuity, boundaries, agency (the sense of being able to act), and centeredness (the sense of being an ongoing enterprise with an identity). Kohut called this stage the *archaic nuclear self—archaic* because the individual is still in a primitive state and *nuclear* because there is now a nucleus (or center).

It is here, in the stage of the archaic self, that Kohut's concepts of idealization and mirroring become manifest. There are actually two aspects to the archaic self—one called the *internal representation of the idealized parent,* or the picture that people have inside of the good and powerful parent who is experienced as part of the self, and the other the *grandiose self*, or the part that demands mirroring and affirmation and is the source of feelings of entitlement.

In healthy maturity, the idealized parents become (or evolve into) a part of us. They are internalized as our *ideals and values*. As individuals, we also internalize certain emotional tasks provided by our parents, such as soothing, modulating anxiety, and providing a sense of ongoingness and cohesion. This, in turn, gives us security by providing us with a sense of identity and the means to maintain a reasonably satisfactory and consistent level of self-esteem. It also helps us to be alone comfortably because our parents are internalized as a part of us. Healthy maturity also changes our primitive need for mirroring (our need to hear how great we are) into realistic ambition.

When our parents are not satisfactorily internalized and this healthy maturity does not develop, narcissistic problems result, as in the case of Clinton. In other words, when individuals, such as Clinton, get stuck in the stage of the grandiose self, or if they retreat back to it (regress) when they are overwhelmed by their problems as adults, they enter a state of *pathological narcissism*. The same is true if the need for mirroring does not evolve into realistic ambition. In this case, the adult endlessly seeks the kind of worshiping adulation that a loving parent gives to an infant. This type of adulation is almost impossible to find in the adult world, so it becomes an unattainable need that leads to an unquenchable thirst and a futile, endless search for that which cannot be had. Clinton's need for mirroring did not evolve into realistic ambition, so we see this dynamic—the constant, futile searching for worshiping adulation—manifest in both his private life and his political life.

Therefore, for Clinton, this process of the archaic self's maturation went awry, leading to a type of "traumatization through omission." In other words, he failed to adequately internalize the idealized parents during early childhood. As a direct result, he was left with "gaps" inside—certain emotional capacities that are weak or lacking, including the ability to self-soothe, modulate anxiety, feel whole, be alone, and feel good about oneself. These internal gaps led Clinton to look outside for something to fill the empty places. The technical name for these gaps is *ego deficits*, and Kohut compared trying to fill them with chemical or behavioral addictions to trying to fill a hole in your stomach by eating food—it simply will not work because the food runs straight through. The hole must be repaired, and the deficit must be made good.

A central characteristic of pathological narcissists, as Kohut understood them, is that they do not treat other people as people in their own right but only as means for them to feel good about themselves. Therefore, their relationships with others are essentially exploitative. We have seen evidence of such exploitative relationships throughout Clinton's life.

As I have written in other books, the psychological aspect of addiction is a regression to the stage of the grandiose self. This is because the grandiose self is the stage in which other people are used exploitatively and in which there is no true separation, or no clear boundary, between the addict and others. The sex addict, for example, views others as existing only to serve him- or herself. Kohut's theory allows us to see that Clinton's addiction has him trapped in the stage of the grandiose self.

Kohut's theory of human development can be applied to understanding not only the emotional stagnation of addicts but also the dynamics of politicians. Politicians are folks who both view themselves idealistically and have exceptionally high needs for mirroring by others. The idealization is manifest in their belief that they are the best and therefore should be elected to office—the belief that they are number one. When reality confirms this, as in the case of a man who is elected president, it is hard to argue that his grandiosity is pathological—after all, the president *is* the most powerful person in the world. Therefore, setting Clinton's idealization of the self aside for the moment, let's concentrate on his need for mirroring, for reflected glory.

It has been said that no one can work a crowd like Bill Clinton. He can make every person he encounters in that crowd feel that they are the center of the world and the sole object of his attention. However, the quid quo pro—the unspoken but understood contract—is that the feeling of being special will be returned, that the person in the crowd that Clinton singles out will feel adulation for him—in fact, that the entire crowd, just like the women in his life, will be seduced by him.

The very emotional survival of a politician of Mr. Clinton's style, who so desperately needs what the crowd gives him, is dependent on the reaction of that crowd. It is not simply political survival, which is readily admitted; it is emotional survival, which is denied, that is at stake in working a crowd.

Now, you may ask, "What is wrong with selling a political program by selling yourself?" It is true that in democratic politics many citizens (whether they care to admit it or not) will vote for a politician on the basis of his or her charm and personality more than his or her political theory or agenda. However, most of us vote for a candidate on the basis of his or her political platform. Herein lies the real problem. Clinton is widely perceived to be a political leader who cannot stand on principle because he is too strongly driven to please the crowd (that is, to do whatever is required to earn their approval) and because he is too caught up in the need to have his greatness mirrored back to him. Because of this aspect of his addictive personality, he swings with the wind, vacillates and reverses, and people-pleases big time. As a result, he has been charged with lacking consistency, being unprincipled, having little integrity, and saying whatever is necessary to get applause and votes. *The same dynamics that drive his addiction also drive his political actions.* We see clearly, time and time again, that Clinton's extreme desire and life-long search for approval has crossed the line from the private to the professional and therefore (because he is the president) has entered the public realm. He tells both individuals and crowds what they want to hear, and in return he expects support, acceptance, and adoration—to hear over and over again, "We love you."

To an extent, this desire to please his constituents is a normal part of politics because, without the support of the citizens, he simply could not get elected and reelected to office. Therefore, on the one hand, the president is expected to *represent* us and our wishes and needs as his constituents; on the other hand, he is also supposed to *direct* us on the basis of his own sound judgment, political expertise, and leadership abilities. Clinton has shown time and time again that he is excellent at meeting our needs (whatever they may be) but, because his need for approval is so consuming, he lacks the abilities to lead and direct us, as a country, into greatness. And greatness is not too much to expect from the man voted into the highest office in the world.

Clinton's idol, John F. Kennedy, struggled with this same problem—the problem of the role of the democratic leader—in his best-seller *Profiles in Courage*. In that book, Kennedy raised a question: To what extent should the democratic leader *reflect* the will of his constituency and to what extent should he *lead* it? Kennedy did not really answer his own question, but he formulated it in a way that would make his readers think about the issue. The men whom he held up as examples in his book were those who did not go with the popular will even though it may have cost them their careers. These men stuck to their beliefs because they had conviction. Bill Clinton, being a voracious reader and admirer of

Kennedy, has certainly read *Profiles in Courage,* yet he has been unable to display the sort of heroic courage and convictions of leadership that Kennedy highlighted.

Instead, Clinton has repeatedly surrendered his own values and beliefs—his own integrity—and, as a result of his unprincipled political style, our country has paid a price. The most egregious example of Clinton's "trimming his sails to go with the wind" was evident during his first term as governor when he capitulated to polluters in his native Arkansas. Clinton ran on a program of environmental reform but quickly realized that he needed money and support from the Arkansas poultry industry (among others), which was rapidly destroying the rivers of that state. Displaying an abysmal lack of integrity, Clinton utterly caved in on the environmental issue to obtain funds and support. Clinton could rationalize his action by saying, "Well, this is the only way I can get reelected, and my political program will certainly be better than my opponents', so it's better to do what I can than to be too idealistic and end up in a position to do nothing." Apparently, he has continued to use essentially similar rationalizations throughout his presidency.

Clinton's ability to rationalize the loss of his own political idealism was strongly reinforced during his work as George McGovern's campaign manager in Texas. McGovern's catastrophic defeat in 1972 taught Clinton a lesson that he never forgot: Never be too far on the left of the American electorate, and never be too idealistic. It is true that to be a pure idealist and to go down in defeat is hardly to advance one's cause. For example, the brilliant socialist idealist Norman Thomas was never elected to office, whereas the pragmatic Franklin Delano Roosevelt was elected president four times. Clinton realized this, and it remains one of the core beliefs deep within his being. Nevertheless, I think that McGovern did more damage to Bill Clinton than Monica Lewinsky ever will. Pragmatism is an admirable strength in politicians, and I am certainly no fan of ideologues or dogmatists; however, for a politician to have convictions yet to remain unable to take a stand and stick to it in terms of any and all issues is a disaster. Such instability results in the inability of the leader to *lead,* and leadership is the most important function of a politician in a democracy.

Clinton's lack of principle was especially evident in his signing of the welfare reform bill just before the 1996 election. He himself described this bill, both before and after signing it, as "cruel" and "immoral." His powerful and repeated strong public statements to this effect are evidence that Clinton believed that the welfare reform bill was flawed and that it would be destructive to human beings. Yet, despite his deep belief in the destructive nature of the bill, Clinton signed it because it was politically expedient to do so. Whether Clinton was right or wrong on the issue is irrelevant—the fact is that he believed that it was an immoral bill, yet he signed it. Clinton could rationalize his action by saying, "Look what kind of government you would have gotten if I hadn't been reelected. It would have been far harsher on welfare recipients than anything that would have come out of my administration, so I did what I had to do to get reelected, and I don't need to apologize for that." This rationalization perfectly parallels his rationalization of capitulating to the polluters in Arkansas. It is a convenient argument that can be used to justify any backing away or straying from principle.

Clinton's flip-flop on gays in the military and his notorious abandonment of his appointees whenever they get into difficulties are further evidence of his "sailing with the wind." During Clinton's 1992 campaign, he vowed to repeal the policy that allowed the Defense Department to seek out, prosecute, and discharge homosexuals serving in the military. Yet, in 1993, in response to intense opposition to the repeal (by both congressional members and the Pentagon), Clinton announced his "Don't ask, don't tell" policy, which in essence continued the policy already in effect.

In January of 1993, Clinton nominated Zoe Baird for attorney general. She withdrew after she was found to have both employed illegal aliens and failed to pay Social Security taxes on them. The following month, Clinton nominated Kimba Woods for the same office. She, too, withdrew when it was discovered that she had employed an undocumented worker.

Clinton's lack of an inner rudder is also apparent in his overreliance on polls. All modern politicians use polling, but not in the way or to the same extent that Clinton does. Not only does Clinton follow the polls more than he leads them, but it has been reported that he takes polls to verify that the public approves of his vacation plans! Ironically, his pollster, Dick Morris, had to be reassigned because of sexual misconduct and is now in a 12-step recovery program for sexual addiction.

At the end of Clinton's first presidential term, when he was in deep political trouble and his reelection doubtful, he compared himself to Harry Truman. Truman was the president who, in 1948, pulled off the biggest upset in American political history when he defeated Thomas Dewey. Aside from the hubris inherent in the comparison—Truman exemplified all that Clinton lacks (courage, inner strength, deeply held and defended convictions, and steadiness of purpose)—Clinton would have done well to remember the act that Truman most regretted and that historians have criticized: his issue of an executive order that set up a loyalty board to investigate "communist leanings" in government employees. Truman issued the order to win the support given the followers of the demagogic Senator Joseph McCarthy. Truman hated McCarthy and all he stood for, and he strongly opposed the anticommunist hysteria of the time. Therefore, by instituting the loyalty program, Truman betrayed his own deepest convictions. The difference was that this was, for Truman, a rare lapse of integrity; however, for Clinton, doing what is expedient and later justifying it has become almost a reflex.

Clinton's compulsive searching for love and approval and his proclivity to base political decisions solely on whether they will get him reelected are closely connected. The overwhelming need for approval, for external confirmation, and for external refutation of all self-doubt and inner pain becomes so powerful that it operates not only in the area of people-pleasing and crowd-pleasing but also as a way to ensure his reelection—the ultimate proof of his worth. Clinton's need is so great that every kind of rationalization can be brought to bear and to justify whatever maneuvering, double-dealing, and turning of his back on principles are necessary to be reelected.

Why the need for such enormous reassurance, unless the yawning doubts within demand constant refutation of the shamefulness within—refutation of that undying core belief of the hurt child that "I'm not worth much," that "I'm not really lovable," that "I have much to be ashamed of," that "I'm responsible for all the bad things that have happened," and that "I'm guilty"? "But no, no, that can't be true, listen to all those people applauding me. Look at all those people voting for me. Listen to all those people praising me. Look at all those people who love me." "No one who is loved in the way that I am loved can be unlovable. It is proof certain that all those self-doubts are nonsense. I can ignore them." This is the same dynamic as the one operative in "All of those women desire me sexually. I must be worthy of their love, their adulation, their passion, their desire for me."

Clinton's waffling on political policy is a result of his need to feel loved, and it is here that we see addiction at work in the political arena. The two dynamics driving political expediency can overlap and interact—doing what one needs to do to get reelected is, of course, a way not only of being a hard-nosed, realistic politician who does whatever is necessary to win but also of guaranteeing that the unconscious, compulsive search for mirroring will be gratified. One feeds the other.

The role of primitive (infantile) idealization in Clinton's dynamics is less clear than the dynamic of mirroring. It could be said that he briefly idealizes the women he seduces, seeing his conquests as the repossession of the idealized mother of his early childhood. Similarly, he may idealize the crowds of supporters, so the crowd who loves him also becomes the all-powerful, all-loving fantasy parent of the toddler. In all fairness, it may also be said that his relationships with men such as Rabin and Brown and his religious involvements and activities have provided healthier outlets for his need to idealize.

Clinton's addictive behavior has also driven his political style in other ways. We have already seen how Clinton's experience as an ACOA, as an Alice Miller kid, makes for a high degree of manipulation and bending of the truth as a result of his lifelong disjunction between what he believes inside and what he presents on the outside. He is so attuned to other people to meet his own needs that he has learned to use that attunement to serve exploitative ends. He has the tools to manipulate and to exploit, and he has applied them from a very early age. He read and befriended his instructors at Georgetown, he charmed the authorities at Oxford, and he has seduced, and continues to seduce, many women, all because he is able to feel his way into other people and experience the world from their points of view. This manipulation and bending of the truth strongly predisposed him to the kind of political shenanigans that Clinton, at his worst, engages in.

Not only a manipulator, President Clinton has also been repeatedly characterized as a liar. Public figures are, of course, not always 100 percent truthful, and I do not have any real way of measuring Bill Clinton's veracity; however, it is only fair to say that for every alleged lie there has been a debate with refutations and counterrefutations, so that the truth remains in question. In addition, Clinton has publicly contradicted himself in more than one circumstance. Again, consider his flip-flopping on the issue of homosexuals in the military, an example that pales in comparison to his waffling on the health-care issue. At the start of his first term, Clinton stated that health-care reform was a major goal of his administration, yet he never came up with a clearly stated plan that he consistently backed. He then hid behind a task force chaired by his wife, whose recommendations he first endorsed and then repudiated. Somehow, he managed to be, almost simultaneously, both in favor of and opposed to every possible plan that emerged.

The great American poet and philosopher Ralph Waldo Emerson wrote, "A foolish consistency is the hobgoblin of little minds," and to some extent this is true. However Clinton is not merely inconsistent; rather, he continually rewrites history, revises his stories, and puts the best possible face on things even when that face distorts reality. In this way, we too have fallen victim to the seduction of Clinton.

There are positive sides to the president's pathology. His warmth, his ability to embrace people, his genuine capacity for empathy in certain situations, and his attempts to bridge the racial gap in this country are also by-products of his compulsion to be liked and admired. Listen to Clinton talk to victims of natural disasters such as floods and hurricanes, and he sounds genuine. This is the best of the people-pleasing Bill Clinton. However, *New York Times* columnist Maureen Dowd made an interesting observation about Bill Clinton during his 1998 visit to Africa. Watching Clinton with Nelson Mandela, she noted that Clinton took on the traits—the very physical mannerisms—of Mandela, just as she had seen him do with other world leaders. She commented that this was beyond empathy and was rather a kind of fusion and loss of identity and, as such, was reminiscent of Woody Allen's *Zelig.* Clinton's tendency to carry identification to the point of merger suggests that he has an identity problem, and both his people-pleasing skills and his addiction are used to self-medicate his *identity diffusion,* that is, his own confusion about who he really is. When he is actively people-pleasing or engaging in sexually addictive behavior, he feels that he has an identity, a cohesive self. To have a president who seems to lack an identity is, to say the least, troublesome. It makes consistent leadership difficult, if not impossible.

To summarize, it may be said that Bill Clinton, like all political leaders and all people, is a mixed bag. Certain aspects of him that find expression in the way he campaigns and governs clearly are connected to being an ACOA, and the very same forces—the underlying need for reassurance and flight from the pain within—drive his sexual addiction. This inner pain, based on ancient shame, is continually reinforced and multiplied by the shame that he feels for both his political and his sexual behavior, so the whole thing becomes an endless, repetitive cycle. To put it simply, the guy needs to be liked and loved too much, and the need is so overwhelming that it undermines all his strengths and assets.

At times, we as citizens have idealized our politicians, just as they have wanted to be. I am well aware that President Clinton lives and functions in a political environment in which adhering to more idealistic social goals is not feasible. He has a Congress of the opposite party and a constituency that is conservative. Although his political stance may appear wishy-washy, it is not nearly as bad as that of other corrupt and double-dealing politicians in American history.

Therefore, although he is hardly a Boss Tweed (the nineteenth-century leader of Tammany Hall who urged democratic voters to "vote early and often") or a Warren Harding (the Republican president whose administration was eventually revealed as the most corrupt in American history), the same dynamics that feed Clinton's addiction have crossed from the private into the professional realm; as a result, we have lost a potentially great leader.

The pathological side of Clinton, the side that is addictive, has led him to unprincipled actions and sudden reversals, bringing up what has been called the "integrity issue of Bill Clinton." The result is that his addiction has made it impossible for him to live up to his potential as a human being or as a president and leader of the world's most powerful nation. Therefore, although it is undeniable that Clinton's addictive behavior has both an upside and a downside, it is equally undeniable that both sides affect us as a nation. It is true that more insight on the part of Clinton would be necessary to help him control the downside, but unfortunately no evidence exists that he is moving in that direction. If Special Prosecutor Kenneth Starr succeeds in bringing Clinton down, all of us will see the tragic consequences—the ultimate self-destructiveness of Clinton's addiction.

CHAPTER SIX

The Path to Self-Destruction

ROS, THE GREEK GOD of erotic love, like all gods, is powerful, mysterious, and even frightening. And, like all gods, he demands the proper form of worship. To ignore his power is to court disaster in the form of self-delusion, self-destructive repression, and an unfulfilled life. Yet, to become Eros's slave is even worse, and those whose worship takes the form of blind submission to his will are even more sorely on the road to self-destruction. The proper worship of this god is to acknowledge the supreme role he plays in our lives without giving him control of our lives. Sexual addiction is worship without restraint—worship that results in bondage and loss of self. This is no less true for the king than for the beggar.

As I have stated elsewhere in this book, people suffering from addictions come from every walk of life, from every socioeconomic class. They sleep in mansions and in gutters. They work in plush offices and on factory floors. They live on virtually every street in the nation. Almost everybody knows one. In my practice I have counseled priests, housewives, doctors, prostitutes, and even a politician or two. I have found that what unites them, aside from their various addictions, is that they carry within themselves the seeds of their own destruction. From the heroin user who shares dirty needles to the gambler who tosses his paycheck into the pot, the consequences of their behavior often leads to broken families, lost careers, and sometimes death.

To understand addiction as inherently self-destructive, it is important to note that all addictions are *biphasic*. Simply put, this means that the development and progression of an addiction consist of two phases. In the first phase, the addict's early experience with the addictive behavior is positive. It brings temporary pleasure, raises self-esteem, and generally works for the addict. However, as the addiction progresses, it turns around and bites the addict in the tail—and it bites hard! When it does, the addict has reached the second phase, and the addiction now causes only pain, making the addict miserable. The chickens have come home to roost. Now, self-destructive feelings and consequences, including guilt, shame, self-hatred, and sometimes disease, divorce, job loss, and other problems flow directly from the addiction. Because this second phase is difficult for the addict to foresee—because the negative consequences are so remote from the earlier positive consequences—the addict falls freely into the trap of self-destruction. Like other sex addicts, Clinton's sexual activities initially brought him pleasure on many different levels (ranging from orgasm to feelings of reassurance, power, and pseudointimacy). Now, however, the consequences are anything but pleasant. For Clinton to see his presidency mired in the muck cannot be especially gratifying.

The question of whether the self-destruction that inevitably accompanies addiction is motivated is hotly debated by addictions specialists. The issue is this: Is the payoff of the addiction "self-punishment"? Or is the self-punishment an unintended consequence of the addiction? Restated: Does the addict *seek* self-destruction at an unconscious or even conscious level? Or is the addict so taken over, so enslaved by his or her addiction, that he or she *has no choice* but to pursue the crack, gambling, drink, or sexual encounter regardless of the consequences? My own view is that these two scenarios are not incompatible. That is, the seeking of self-punishment can be part of the motivation for addiction *and* it may be the case that, after a certain point, motivation becomes irrelevant—the addict cannot help him- or herself any longer.

Harvard psychiatrist Edward Khantzian has argued that addictions serve the purpose of self-medication and that they are driven by emotional pain and a mistaken and misguided attempt to alleviate that pain. Others view addicts as pleasure seekers—impulsive, grandiose, and uncaring of consequences. Yet others, such as renowned psychiatrist Karl Menninger, have called addictions "chronic suicide" that is driven by guilt and the need for self-punishment. I think they are all correct—every addiction is driven by emotional pain and the need to alleviate it, pleasure seeking, a lack of (or poor) impulse control, grandiosity, and self-destructiveness. The bottom line is that motivated or not, the inevitable outcome of an unarrested addiction is self-destruction. This might be obvious in the case of an addiction like alcoholism but is no less true of the behavioral addictions such as sexual addiction.

As previously noted in Chapter One, Clinton does not appear to be *motivated* by self-destruction, yet, because his addiction has progressed, he has reached the point where the potential to self-destruct is now evident. Later in this chapter, we examine what self-destruction might look like for Clinton. First, though, let's see what self-destruction has looked like for other addicts.

Remember that addicts (unless they are sociopaths) feel intense guilt over their addictive behavior. By continuing their addictive behavior, addicts temporarily dull the pain caused by guilt, and, because the addiction now brings more pain than pleasure, they are simultaneously engaging in a form of self-punishment. Self-punishment, by its very nature, is destructive, and the resulting damage can manifest in many forms. The following case illustrates what self-destruction was for Sam.

A highly successful businessman, Sam owned a trucking company, drove expensive sports cars, and lived in a million-dollar home. He was also a cocaine addict. Sam came to me for treatment after he ran into trouble with the Internal Revenue Service. The IRS had attached many of his assets, and he feared criminal prosecution. Unfortunately, his therapy sessions with me ultimately turned out to be a waste of time. Sam was certain that his wealth would solve all his problems, including his wife's threat to leave him. It didn't. Within a year, he lost his business, his sports cars, his home, and his wife. The more he lost, the more he needed to get high on cocaine, and the more he got high on cocaine, the more he lost. He was so out of control that his only chance for recovery was to enter an inpatient rehabilitation center. I tried in every way I knew to convince Sam to admit himself, but he refused. His grandiosity and angry defiance ("I can *buy* my way out of this!") prevented him from hearing me. To let down this defense would expose Sam to more pain than he believed he could endure; yet only by experiencing the full tragedy of his traumatic downfall could he be helped. Because he could not face the pain, he fled—simply disappeared—walking away from the remnants of his crumbled empire.

Dr. S. was also destroyed by his addiction. A busy internist, he made having sex a condition of employment in his office. As the years went on, he took more and more risks, at one point having oral sex with his nurses as he went from examining room to examining room. As his behavior became less and less controlled, his practice started to dwindle, and his wife left him. In a way similar to the public's reaction to Clinton's sexual proclivities, some patients disregarded Dr. S.'s "problem" because he was so skillful an internist; however, most did not. Most of his patients probably did not know *exactly* what was wrong, but they knew enough to sense that Dr. S.'s office was not a happy place. Before long, his income dropped to the point where he found it difficult to meet his expenses. To make matters worse, no one wanted to work for him. Dependent on his nurses for multiple tasks, he started to panic. As Dr. S. became more anxious, fearing abandonment by both clientele and staff, he needed more sex than ever, and soon he was picking up women in bars. Dr. S. lost his family (when his wife discovered him in bed with another woman), his reputation, his professional standing, and a large part of his income. His self-destruction was virtually complete. Eventually, he shut down his office and joined the Army. This was his attempt at what A.A. calls a *geographic cure*—physically running away from one's problems without ever facing them, without ever relinquishing denial and getting help for one's addiction. Unfortunately, joining the service in midlife was unlikely to stop his precipitous plunge.

For some individuals, self-destruction comes not only in the demise of a marriage or the death of a career. For some, self-destruction comes in the form of *physical* death. The following case illustrates this.

The Path to Self-Destruction

Dr. M. was a world-famous psychiatrist, author of a standard textbook, professor at a top medical school, and president of numerous professional organizations. Although he was both disliked (for his autocratic ways) and distrusted (because his theoretical allegiances swayed with the trends), he was still successful and respected. Dr. M. was also a sex addict who abused his female patients by taking advantage of the power differential. Hitting on a symptom-ridden patient is not only an abuse of trust and an exploitation of the *transference*—the emotional bond between a patient and a doctor—but also the use of a status differential to get into someone's pants. This abuse of power echoes Clinton's behavior with Monica Lewinsky. Dr. M. went even further and had sex with some of his patients while they were drugged. Late in his career, a former patient filed a lawsuit.

After the suit was filed, one female patient after another came forward, accusing Dr. M. of having had sex with them unethically both by violating medical ethics by seducing them while they were in analysis with him and by having sex with some patients while they were sedated. He denied it all, claiming that his former patients were "out to get me." An otherwise healthy man, Dr. M. died not long after his reputation had been destroyed. Disgrace and emotional stress directly related to addiction can be just as fatal as a drug overdose, AIDS, other infectious diseases, or the violent situations in which addicts often find themselves. Dr. M.'s death was certainly related to the complete devastation and shame he experienced.

Intended or not, his sexual addiction led to his self-destruction, the seeds of which were planted long before his death.

Kevin had once been a high-powered account executive in one of the largest advertising agencies in Chicago, but snorting $200,000 up his nose in the form of cocaine had changed that. In addition to his cocaine addiction, Kevin had a secondary addiction to women. Although not a sex addict in the usual sense, he needed to always have a woman taking care of him. Abandoned by his mother as a child, he manipulated other women into supporting him in an effort to replace the mother he lost as a child. In fact, the unconscious need to make himself a helpless infant needing to be "nursed" was one of the most powerful dynamics driving his cocaine addiction and the relentless destruction of his career, his economic security, and his place in the world.

By the time I met him, he had become a street person. He had been dumped by his latest "sugar mommy" and had attempted to sue his estranged wife for a financial settlement. One of the couple's few remaining assets was an expensive condominium, and Kevin had asked for half its value. When the case went to trial, his wife took the stand and testified that the value of the condo was greatly reduced because Kevin had trashed it during one of his "cocaine manias." At that point, Kevin interrupted his wife's testimony, stating in a pathetic, pleading little boy's voice, "But, your Honor, the only damage I ever did to that apartment was caused when the hook pulled out of the ceiling when I tried to hang myself." Biting her lip to keep from laughing, the judge called the court to order. Kevin did eventually get a substantial settlement, but the money did not last long. Although he denied it, some of the money most likely went for cocaine, and in a short time he was back on the streets. This was a man who once supervised others and had respect, success, and a good deal of money. Now he had nothing. Whether his life was shattered by his cocaine addiction, by his dependency conflict, or by both (as is most likely), the self-destructiveness of his addiction destroyed him.

All four of the men just discussed were powerful professionals, and each self-destructed as a result of his addiction. By taking unnecessary risks and acting in an arrogant, grandiose manner, each of these men ruined the successful life he once lived. What happens when the addict who is self-destructing is not only a powerful professional but an *elected official*—a public *leader*?

Men who achieve political power naturally have high levels of energy, tremendous aggressiveness, and a relentless pursuit of dominance. Nothing is surprising about that behavior carrying over from the political realm to the private, specifically the sexual, realm. However, *true leaders are programmed to lead, not to self-destruct,* and when a political leader has a sexual addiction, the self-destructive nature of that addiction undermines his leadership abilities. Herein lies the important difference between President Clinton and other presidents who have had extramarital affairs.

Many writers have tried to rationalize and justify Clinton's sexual behavior on the grounds that many other presidents have been unfaithful to their wives. Presidents as varied as Lyndon B. Johnson, Franklin Delano Roosevelt, Dwight D. Eisenhower, and John F. Kennedy immediately come to mind as powerful leaders who have strayed from their marriage vows. In what way were their affairs different from Clinton's? The answer is that *their private indiscretions were not self-destructive and did not compromise their leadership skills.*

President Roosevelt was unfaithful to his wife, Eleanor, a woman who disliked sex and who told her daughter Anna that it was something women had to endure. Eleanor would have agreed with the Victorian-era mother who told her daughter on the eve of her wedding, "Close your eyes and think of England." Franklin and Eleanor loved each other deeply, but Franklin dealt with his wife's reported distaste for sex by having an affair with her social secretary, Lucy Mercer.

Naturally, when Eleanor learned about the affair, she was devastated, but the couple decided to remain married (after Franklin vowed never to see Mercer again), largely to protect Franklin's political future. He kept his word for many years, but, when his health was failing and the burdens of his presidency became overwhelming, his daughter Anna arranged for him to once again spend time with Mercer (now a widow). When the president died in the presence of his mistress at Warm Springs, Georgia, Eleanor was once again wounded to the core. So, Roosevelt, like Clinton, was a presidential leader who was not faithful to his wife. Why should we be more concerned about Clinton's affairs than Roosevelt's? Despite the sad, even tragic, nature of this story, the important difference between Roosevelt and Clinton is simple. During his presidency, Roosevelt kept his private life private, never allowing it to cross the line into the public realm and therefore affect his leadership abilities. Because he had better control of his sexual impulses and because he was better able to keep his private life private, Roosevelt's affair (although it deeply hurt his wife) neither interfered with his ability to lead the nation nor resulted in any type of self-destruction.

President Eisenhower, one of the greatest wartime commanders, was a man extremely in control and of great probity. During the war, he too had girlfriend, Kay Summersby. After the war, Kay wrote a best-selling book, *My Boss Ike,* which indirectly stated that she and Ike had been lovers. However, as soon as the war had ended, Ike went back to his wife, Mamie, and that was the end of that. Unlike Clinton, Eisenhower's great leadership skills had not been compromised by his extramarital affair.

President Johnson was known to have had many affairs. When First Lady Ladybird was asked about them, her comment was, "Well, Lyndon loved people, and women are more than half of people." Both Ladybird and Johnson himself viewed his sexual proclivities as a kind of rogueness that, unlike Clinton's behavior, was carefully kept out of the public light until well after his death. Johnson, by keeping his extracurricular sex life private, was never forced to spend the enormous time and energy that Clinton spends defending himself. Like Eisenhower and Roosevelt before him, Johnson's sexual activities never seriously hindered his ability to function as a public servant, nor did they contain the necessary elements that could lead to his downfall.

It has been said that Clinton's private life is public only because we, as a nation, have lost the ability to be civil in our public discourse and because his enemies, abated by a prurient press, have microscopically scrutinized every facet of his personal life and magnified it to huge proportions. It is true that the world has changed since Roosevelt, Eisenhower, and Johnson were in office. First, social attitudes about sex have changed. Sex has permeated social consciousness, largely through the media. Today, it is everywhere you look—in advertisements, movies, novels, television, magazines, and now on the Internet. In addition, women's roles in the workplace have changed. More and more independent women are in the workforce, and most of these women demand equal treatment. These parallel movements have brought new and important issues to bear. For example, what does (and does not) constitute inappropriate sexual behavior? Sexual harassment laws have been enacted and are enforced in the workplace. Today's women are not afraid to speak out when inappropriate sexual advances take place. Previously, women had to put up with such advances if they wanted to remain employed, but no longer. Now there is legal recourse against such mistreatment.

Like all social changes, this movement has its downside. Some women are driven by vindictiveness, power needs, greed, or all these. Many of these women take advantage of the newfound status and social awareness to terrorize and intimidate men to the point that the workplace becomes infused with suspicion and paranoia. In its own way, this is as undesirable as the old abuses, in which women were always on the receiving end of the exploitation. It is possible (although *I* do not believe it for a minute) that Clinton may yet turn out to be the victim that he says he is and wind up a hero to men who believe that they, too, have been victimized by the changing roles that define relations between the sexes.

Nevertheless, the question remains: Given the change in social attitudes about sex and considering that women during other presidencies were undoubtedly more passive, does Clinton "look bad" only because today's women speak out? To put the question differently, is Clinton simply no different than other presidents who had extramarital affairs? No, he *is* different. You simply cannot write off Clinton's behavior by stating that he is just like other presidents and that only because he is living in this day and age does his behavior look worse, that is, more self-destructive.

A comparison with cigarette smoking might be instructive. Thirty years ago, the fact that a person smoked did not imply anything about his or her personality or propensity to addiction. It was simply what people did. This is no longer true. Because of what we know about the health risks and dangers, social attitudes about smoking have changed. If you smoke today in full knowledge of the health risks it carries, it does say something about your personality and propensity to addiction. It says that something in you leads you to engage in a behavior known to be socially disapproved of and self-destructive and that something is more powerful than your rational side. You cannot argue that Clinton is doing what the other presidents did. The other presidents lived and worked in a different time and social context. Things are simply not the same, and, "as our case is new, we must think anew," and so must our current and future presidents think and behave anew. The president of the United States must change and adapt to keep up with the times.

It is also true that today's media are far less respectful of the private lives of public figures, and the sex lives of the powerful, rich, and famous are grist for reputable news programs as well as the tabloid news and talk shows. One hears claims that the country is losing potential future leaders because no one in their right mind would want to subject themselves to such intrusion and hostile publicity. A recent *New York Times* article highlighted the difficulty both Republicans and Democrats are having finding credible candidates to run for Congress in the November 1998 elections. No one wants to be scrutinized in the way that Clinton is being scrutinized, and undoubtedly Clinton's private life is being examined in a way that it would not have been examined a generation or less ago. Investigative reporting has acquired a hard edge and an obsessive quality of its own.

Had today's media existed during the other presidencies, those men may well have been exposed much like Clinton. Although we can only speculate whether other presidents would have curtailed their behavior had their affairs broken into the public light, the compassionate assertion that poor Clinton operates in a "different time and place" remains weak as a justification of Clinton and his behavior. Clinton is well-aware of how today's press operates, and he was repeatedly warned early by friends and advisors when his sexual indiscretions started to become public knowledge. Yet, he still refused, or was unable, to stop the behavior. Therefore, although the times have changed, bringing new attitudes about sex and a more invasive press, it appears to be common knowledge that a president simply cannot philander any longer and get away with it. Everyone seems to know this—everyone, that is, except for Clinton.

Unlike the other presidents we discussed, we see Clinton risking everything to have sexual affairs—to feed his addiction. Fully cognizant of the fact that he was under media scrutiny and aware that the media were "researching" every aspect of his personal life, Clinton nevertheless chose to make sexual advances toward Gennifer Flowers and Paula Jones. Even after he was aware that Special Prosecutor Kenneth Starr was poised to destroy him, he nonetheless allegedly made advances toward Kathleen Willey and Monica Lewinsky. He opened the door and invited both personal and political destruction. In fact, he has danced with self-destruction throughout his career in public service, while Hillary (at least in the public eye) has remained strongly and warmly supportive of her husband throughout. Whether motivated by love, a sincere belief in her husband's innocence, her own power drive, or her own emotional needs to enable, Hillary has been most voracious in her attacks on the special prosecutor and strident in her condemnation of what she claims is a "vast right-wing conspiracy," a conspiracy that she alleges is determined to hunt down and destroy her husband.

The conservative journalist David Brock, who first brought the lurid details about the State Troopers to light, has since apologized to the president. However, his apology did not retract the content of what he wrote. Rather, it cast doubt on the reliability of his informants: four Arkansas State Troopers. The troopers are alleged to have received money from an extreme right-wing group. This same group allegedly financed the production of the Reverend Jerry Falwell's video that purported to prove that Clinton was linked to the murder of former Assistant White House Council Vincent Foster (the death of whom law enforcement agencies have ruled a suicide).

Regardless of whether such a right-wing conspiracy exists, Clinton (like every powerful political leader) has enemies, and undoubtedly those seeking to destroy him have spent large amounts of money to dig up dirt and damaging information. However, it is crystal clear that neither side could exist without the other. On the one hand, the intense hostility of Clinton's enemies naturally triggers Clinton's denial and defensiveness. On the other hand, if Clinton had not made himself vulnerable, his opponents would have little to do. Instead, Clinton's risky, self-destructive behavior has provided his critics with ample ammunition to use against him. He has fed, and he continues to feed, his opponents exactly what they are hungry for. It is somewhat like the cops needing the robbers and vice versa. The robbers would not have nearly so much fun if no cops were there to outwit.

Despite the differences between Clinton and the other presidents, the one president in American history whom, in retrospect, Clinton appears to strongly resemble is John F. Kennedy. In fact, Clinton's similarities to Kennedy, another leader now known to have had extramarital affairs, are rather striking. Kennedy was Clinton's role model and hero from the time Clinton met him on a trip to Washington as a "senator from Arkansas" (during the Boys Nation annual mock government expedition). To have been selected to go on the trip was an early political triumph for Clinton, who never forgot his meeting with Kennedy. One could argue that by no accident did Clinton choose (consciously or unconsciously) to model himself after a man renowned for his charms with women, a man who was compulsive in his own sex life. In fact, Kennedy's sexual behavior had a profound influence on Clinton, even foreshadowing Clinton's behavior in many ways.

Kennedy was unabashedly unfaithful, and, unlike other presidents (yet similar to Clinton), he became involved in high-risk situations. For example, Kennedy's reputed sharing of women with various gangsters was clearly outrageous, risky, and dangerous and, in hindsight, might have bordered on the self-destructive. For Kennedy, the risk taking seems to have been part of the "kick" of his sexual involvements. He appeared to have received intense pleasure from being in potentially compromising situations. By taking such risks, he was, in a way, thumbing his nose at the world. Kennedy's affair with Hollywood star Marilyn Monroe was much like his father's affair with another Hollywood celebrity, Gloria Swanson. Similarly, Clinton's pursuit of women parallels that of his own biological father. Just as we cannot say (with any certainty) whether Kennedy would have self-destructed as a result of dangerous and risky sexual behavior, we cannot predict if, when, or how Clinton will self-destruct.

So far, Clinton is fighting tenaciously to survive, and he will probably do so. If Clinton *were* to self-destruct, what might it look like? His self-destruction could take form publicly and politically, privately, or both. If Starr can prove that Clinton is guilty of obstruction of justice, the House of Representatives would be forced to start impeachment proceedings. Even if those proceedings eventually went nowhere (which probably would be the case), Clinton's presidency would be indelibly stained, and his effectiveness as a leader would almost certainly come to an end. We do not yet know how the consequences of Clinton's sexually addictive behavior will play out in his private life. It is possible that Hillary will divorce him once he leaves office. We also cannot be sure what the long-term effects will be on his relationship with his daughter. And, at another subtle, inward level, we do not know what effect the current scandals will have on Clinton's relationship with himself.

The Path to Self-Destruction

Clinton's potential for self-destruction is illuminated when one considers his reaction following President Richard Nixon's death. Clinton was inexplicably grief ridden and led an unusually (and some may say, inappropriately) prolonged period of public mourning for Nixon—a self-destructed president driven from office by fear of almost certain impeachment. How much of Clinton's actions are the result of a conscious or unconscious identification with Nixon? At some level, Clinton *must* understand the possible consequences of his reckless behavior. He must know that he is walking a tightrope and is one misstep away from disaster. Perhaps somewhere in his being he fears that that misstep is inevitable, that the seeds of his own destruction, motivated or not, cannot lie fallow forever. At an unconscious level, that may even be the reason behind the enthusiasm he developed for Nixon, a disgraced president of the opposition party whose political aims and values were quite different from his own.

It seems almost that Clinton anticipated his own public disgrace and the recriminations he has suffered and that, with uncanny and unconscious instinct, he has linked himself to a president who came close to impeachment and was forced to resign. Did Clinton somehow know that he, like Nixon, would sail into his second term flying high and then rapidly find himself in deep trouble? Yes, Clinton's self-destructive part bound him to Nixon and resulted in his overpraising the dead president. In this, as in his identification with Kennedy, Clinton seems to anticipate his future—glory followed by a tragic fall to unknown depths.

Whether or not Clinton self-destructs, damage has been done. As much as the American people continue to support the president—a support based equally on his charm, persuasiveness, and the nation's continuing prosperity—Clinton's presidency, in many ways, has become an embarrassment for all of us. He is the only president whose alleged penile irregularities have been the subject of a lawsuit and voluminous discussions in the press. The whole business around his sex life is poisoning American politics, demeaning the office of the presidency, and frightening people away from the public sphere.

I cannot help but wonder whether Clinton has hit bottom. As far as we know, Lewinsky is the last name on his current doomsday list. However, on the basis of my years of experience in treating addictions, I would speculate that Clinton is currently controlling his behavior because he is too frightened to do otherwise and that he has not really relinquished his denial. If this is the case, he remains vulnerable and might yet take that final and fatal step, get involved with another woman, become mired in yet another scandal, and end his presidency in disgrace. If he does, his identification with Nixon will be complete.

PART TWO

Regaining Control: The Recovery Process

CHAPTER SEVEN

The Long, Difficult Road Back

I HAVE ARGUED THROUGHOUT THIS book that addiction is a futile attempt to fill an inner emptiness. It just plain does not work. The key to all addictions lies in the fact that the addict is looking for something outside that can be found only inside. The tragedy is that everything that the addict so desperately seeks in compulsion and consumption is somewhere inside the individual. Surprisingly, this is true despite all that is missing as a result of faulty development and despite all that has been lost in the course of the addiction itself.

Bill Clinton's continued sexual behavior is prima facie evidence that winning all those elections—from high school class president to the various class offices at Georgetown and Oxford to attorney general, to governor, and to president—have not done anything to make him feel better about himself.

No number of elections won or any plurality in those elections can fill the hole. No amount of working the crowd can do it, either. This is truly tragic because the part of Bill Clinton that is so driven, that is so people-pleasing that he is perceived to be a liar and manipulator, is also the part of Bill Clinton that at times genuinely reaches people and touches them. Therefore, one of his greatest strengths is spoiled, and his gift for communicating becomes a curse: "If they don't like me, I will cease to exist. My only hope is to work another crowd, seduce another woman, or win another election." The trouble with this is that no possibility exists of just being "okay" by simply being—of feeling whole and somehow alright, even if the crowd does not applaud, even if the woman will not have sex with him.

No one has such secure self-esteem that he or she is immune to the slings and arrows of outrageous fortune; and, of course, we feel better about ourselves when we get that promotion, when other people like us, and when we win elections, but that is not the point. The point is that depending on those kinds of experiences for any kind of self-esteem is holding oneself hostage to fate, and that, in the end, is crippling.

Now that we know what will *not* work for Clinton, we are left with a question: "What *will* work?" What could Clinton do to break free from his addictive behavior? For that matter, what can anyone do to recover from such an all-consuming problem?

Quite a few options exist for those seeking to recover from sexual addiction, including 12-step programs and non-12-step self-help programs as well as a variety of therapeutic approaches. Within these treatment options are top-down approaches and bottom-up approaches. Top-down approaches require that the addict first stop the behavior and then examine the thoughts and feelings that emerge. The belief is that only then can the addict understand and gain control over the internal feelings and emotions that drive the addiction. The insight gained after the addictive behavior is controlled will in turn prevent the addict from returning to the behavior. Bottom-up approaches do not seek to stop the addictive behavior initially; rather, they seek to identify the underlying forces in the hope that recognizing what causes the addiction will help the addict control his or her behavior. This type of psychotherapy, called *psychodynamic therapy* or *insight therapy*, helps people explore who they are and how they got to be that way and often leads to excellent results. An advantage of this kind of therapy is that the patient is not expected to be "well" (in the sense that he or she has given up the behavior) before treatment can begin. In these cases, the therapist has time to develop a rapport and trust with the patient before asking for behavioral change.

The two approaches are not incompatible because the goal remains the same; the difference lies only in emphasis. Just like the bottom-up approach, the top-down approach *does* seek to understand motivational factors, but not initially. Likewise, just like the top-down approach, the bottom-up approach *does* seek to help the patient stop the addictive behavior, but again not initially.

Many argue that the bottom-up approach does not work with addictions and that it is far more effective to take the top-down approach. Like most addictions specialists, I generally agree that the top-down approach is best, but the important point is that recovery take place, no matter how it is done.

It is significant that both approaches at some point deal with the underlying dynamics of the addiction, specifically because the dynamic of anesthetizing or self-medicating through an addiction often masks both buried emotions and serious psychiatric disorders. These psychiatric disorders, when coexisting with an addiction, are called *comorbidities,* and they must be addressed if one is to recover. Comorbidities include clinical depression (ranging from a chronic minor form, *dysthmia,* to major depression and manic depression); anxiety disorders, including generalized anxiety, panic disorder, various phobias, and obsessive-compulsive disorder; posttraumatic stress disorder; and attention-deficit disorder. Attempts at self-medicating psychiatric disorders by engaging in addictive behavior always fail sooner or later (most often sooner), so it is imperative that the person suffering a comorbidity get help for the comorbid condition. For example, you are unlikely to overcome your sexual addiction until your depression is addressed and treated if your behavior serves as your only way of medicating your depression.

Psychiatrist Ariel Goodman conceptualizes the treatment of sexual addiction as a three-stage process: (1) behavioral—controlling the addiction, (2) dynamic—treating the underlying addictive process, and (3) pharmacological—treating the depression and anxiety that the compulsion was self-medicating. The behavioral part is accomplished by participating in 12-step programs such as Sexual Compulsives Anonymous and by training in relapse prevention. The dynamic part is accomplished through psychotherapy aimed at uncovering shame and traumatic memories. The pharmacological part is accomplished by taking drugs such as Prozac. I have found that this three-part approach works extremely well for addicts who choose recovery.

It is important to note that those who do choose to get help for their addictions have taken the first step toward a better life simply by making the decision to recover. However, recovery from sexual addiction is complicated by many factors. First, consider the contrast between addiction to narcotics and addiction to sex. There is no such thing as "healthy" use of cocaine or heroin (however strenuously their devotees might disagree), but there is "healthy" sex. As complex as sexual behavior and its evaluation might be, there is a core of commonly held beliefs about what does and does not constitute healthy sex. For example, most people believe that sex should not be primarily about trying to heal childhood wounds, filling gaps left by unfortunate developmental experiences, anesthetizing feelings (such as anger, shame, or insecurity), or creating diversions and distractions from the reality of one's life. In reality, sex occasionally fills some of these functions for virtually everyone, but they should not be the main motivators of sexual behavior.

Most people will also agree that sex should be about sex and, with the right person, also about love. It should be either spontaneous fun—something that feels good and is worthwhile in and of itself—or one of the most powerful and deeply communicative experiences in life. These are not incompatible; in fact, one experience can serve both purposes. Sometimes sexual spontaneity and ecstasy have nothing to do with deep communication, and at other times it is about as close to melting into oneness as people get. For most human beings, the experience of sexual union is as close as they will ever get to realizing what mystics of many cultures describe as "becoming one with the totality of things."

Despite the fact that few will argue these ideas, the notion of healthy sex remains subjective, causing problems for individuals trying to identify what recovery might "look like" for them. Is healthy sex only heterosexual monogamy? Does it include homosexual monogamy, or might it include various arrangements in which monogamy is not an absolute requirement? Should there not be a provision for the person who does not have a partner but who is still entitled to a sex life?

Simply because one engages in a form of sexual behavior that is different from the old ideal of monogamous heterosexuality does not make that individual a sex addict. Different personal tastes and situations make different forms of sexual behavior appropriate to one's life circumstances. Pinning a scarlet letter on everyone whose sexual behavior does not match our own not only is cruel but also results in nothing but judgment, conceal- ment, and hypocrisy. And although some people enjoy disparaging others, especially if there is a psychiatric jus- tification for doing so, it is not productive for anyone, in- cluding the person doing the judging. Therefore, no globally accepted definition for healthy sex exists, and finding the right balance is very difficult.

Another complicating factor is recognizing *when* re- covery from sexual addiction has occurred. Again, con- sider cocaine and heroin addicts. Cocaine addicts know that they are recovering if they are not snorting cocaine. Heroin addicts know that they are in recovery if they are not shooting up heroin. For these addicts, it is a black- and-white situation. Now consider this: How does a sex addict know that he or she is recovering? As long as they are not having sex? Not necessarily. We have already rec- ognized that sex is a natural part of our lives, and be- cause healthy sex exists and is desirable (although it can mean different things to different people), complete ab- stinence is rarely if ever the goal of recovery. Therefore, although abstinence is not the *end* goal, is it necessary for recovery? If so, for how long?

Some recovery groups and therapists recommend a period of abstinence for those in recovery. The idea is to get away from the addiction and those things that trigger it altogether. This also helps the addict learn that sex, no matter how important it might be, is not a biological necessity—that, although as a species we need it to survive, as individuals we do not. The cover of the sex education handbook once published by the McGill University student government read, "Sex is never an emergency." This is true. Sex might feel like an emergency, but it never truly is.

Although it is often is recommended, not everyone who recovers from sexual addiction has done so by going through a period of abstinence. My own feeling is that abstinence is a good idea. It puts things into perspective and gives the recovering person a sense of mastery.

Recovering from sexual addiction is complicated further by the fact that sexual addiction, like all forms of addiction, is a form of slavery. Addicts are, in essence, slaves to their addictions because the addictions take over their lives to the point where they feel powerless to stop the behavior and also lose their authority and freedom of choice in all areas of life. Therefore, because of the enslaving nature of addictions, addicts are able to avoid or flee from the responsibilities that come with freedom. This is illustrated in psychologist Erich Fromm's book *Escape from Freedom,* which examines the dynamics of totalitarian societies such as Nazi Germany and Soviet Russia. Fromm concludes that the psychological base of the mass support of those states was a desire to escape from the consequences of being free. He hypothesized that it was easier for individuals to have someone else in command and control because then they did not need to be responsible for their actions: "I'm only following orders—everything is determined for me." The same is true whether the dictator be heroin or a sexual compulsion. Addiction as slavery is not a remarkable notion. What is surprising is that addicts actually *desire* to be enslaved to escape the sheer terror of making choices (of being in control of their own lives). Therefore, although being enslaved (like an addict) is a horrible experience, from the perspective of the addict it has its good points. If you do not believe me, read the book of Exodus in the Bible. Over and over again, the freed Hebrew slaves rebel against Moses and want to go back to the slavery and the "fleshpots" of Egypt. This has been the experience of every revolutionary leader.

The existential philosopher Søren Kierkegaard wrote about the "dizziness of freedom." This dizziness results when people realize that they are free and responsible for their actions. It engenders enormous anxiety in them, and they might be tempted to flee by enslaving themselves in one way or another—whether it be to a political state, a religious cult (such as that of David Koresh), or a chemical or behavioral addiction. In this way, it could be said that sexual addiction does not leave a person many choices, and the addict recognizes this.

My years of clinical practice have verified that addictions are ways of fleeing responsibility. I have found that any recovering addicts who look back at their lives (during the period in which they were actively addicted) will readily tell you that it was slavery and, with a little introspection, that as horrible as it was, there was something about it they liked, just as prisoners grow to like their cells. Plato's myth of the cave tells about slaves who were chained in a cave. When they were released, they ventured outdoors, but were so blinded by the sunlight that they ran back into the cave. Plato's myth of the cave is the story of many a relapse. When addicts are recovering—whether from sexual addiction or any other addiction—there comes a period when they realize, "I can. I can leave my wife, I can change jobs, I can go to an ashram. I am free. I have choices." And that realization is both thrilling and terrifying.

What else can complicate recovery from sexual addiction? Many sex addicts have more than one addiction, a condition called a *polyaddiction* or *cross-addiction*. For example, in addition to sex, they might have an addiction to alcohol, drugs, or other behavioral addictions (such as compulsive gambling or compulsive overeating). This makes recovery difficult because the addict must battle more than one addiction. Although we do not have good prevalence figures on sexual addiction, we do know something about the rates of cross-addiction. Of all the known people considered to be sex addicts, about 42 percent are cross-addicted to drugs and alcohol and many others are cross-addicted to food, spending, work, or gambling.

Although each case must be evaluated individually and the totality of the polyaddict's situation taken into account, I generally favor dealing with one addiction at a time. Trying to accomplish too much too soon might be setting oneself up for failure. As such, an overzealous approach to recovery might be a way to ensure that one recovers from nothing.

Recovery is complicated further by another problem: the traumatic nature of being out of control. Being out of control causes panic, and situations in which panic exists are traumatic. Although not all addicts have been traumatized in childhood, most have. In the case of those who have been traumatized, the trauma caused by the addiction itself becomes superimposed on the unresolved traumas of childhood. The new traumatization makes it extremely difficult to work through prior traumatizations and to come to terms with the injuries of one's childhood.

Therefore, it is evident that many factors must be overcome if one is to recover from a sexual addiction. Sometimes addicts are able to conquer these obstacles; at other times they are not.

Reverend Smith came to me both angry and desperate. He had a cross-addiction to alcohol and drugs and came from a childhood filled with traumatic events. It was a strange session because he did not let me get a word in edgewise.

Doctor, I don't want to be here. God should be enough, and it really pisses me off to have to see you.

I'm a recovering alcoholic and drug addict, but my congregation doesn't know, and I live in fear that someone will see me at one of the Alcoholics Anonymous meetings I attend out of town. I know this is foolish because they would only think the more of me if they knew I had overcome my addictions. Until the other day I hadn't had an affair for two years, but it has been the only thing on my mind. Doctor, I have a pattern. I don't have affairs for two-year periods, and I also stay sober, but then I go out again. The real problem is the sex. I'm not satisfied with my marriage. My wife gave me oral sex when we were engaged and now she won't. It infuriates me. I've been cheated—it was just false advertising. Sometimes, I see someone in my congregation and I really want to do it with them. I've never had much trouble getting them either. But each time I do, I get tormented with guilt and wind up drinking. I just can't seem to put more than two sober years together in spite of going to A.A. There's a woman whose child is in my confirmation class. Well, I did screw her, when I got her in my study last week, and now if the past is prelude, I'm going to be drinking in a few days. I told my A.A. sponsor about it, but it doesn't really help. I just can't stand the guilt.

Last week I was officiating at an interfaith dinner. The Presbyterian minister is really hot, and as I was giving my sermon, all I could think about was getting in her pants. A few times I almost said something inappropriate because I wasn't even thinking about what I was supposed to be saying.

The damn problem is that since I've been in recovery I feel guilty about screwing the ladies in my congregation. I never did before. When I was drinking I had sex all the time, it felt great, and I had no guilt. When I was using heroin I had what was called "dope dick." That means I could stay hard forever and women loved it. But now dammit I have trouble, and I don't know if I want to be faithful to my wife or not—I don't like the fact that she doesn't perform oral sex anymore. But I know if I get the Presbyterian minister, I'm going to be off and running—getting drunk and high all the time. The last time I had an affair, I lost my job and wound up in another rehab. My wife said if I slip again she is finished. We have three children, and I do not want to lose them. Dammit doctor—all I can think about is having sex! When I read the Bible, all I think about is sex; when I'm giving a sermon, all I can think about is sex. Even when I'm not doing it, I think about it.

My father was nuts. He was a minister too but he could never hold a job, so he ended up becoming a sexton. We were poor, and to make it worse, he was fanatically cheap. He was always screaming not to play the radio because we would wear it out and crazy stuff like that. My mother is a doormat. As soon as I hit my teens I discovered booze and pot, and before long I was doing hard drugs too, but the main thing has always been sex. As long as I was getting sex, I was okay.

The Reverend Smith assumed that the women would never "tell," although subconsciously he feared they would. It turned out that the reverend had been sexually abused as a child. He had been seduced as an adolescent by one of the women in his father's church and earlier had been sexually abused by a man who was also a member of his father's congregation. Everything about being a minister was sexualized for him. But the most powerful force driving him was the defense mechanism we saw in Clinton's life—the act of "turning the passive into the active," of doing to instead of being done to. Recall that it is the need to endlessly repeat a traumatic event to gain mastery over it, a futile attempt to feel in control. Freud called it *repetition compulsion:* "We act instead of remembering." In this context, *remembering* does not refer only to an intellectual or cognitive memory but to an emotional or affective memory as well—to remember with *feeling.* My piano teacher, having a hopelessly inept pupil, would say in desperation, "Once more with *feeling.*" To escape the endless cycle of reenactment, to escape enslavement to the repetition of compulsion, the addict must play it once more with feeling.

Reverend Smith was highly exploitative in his sexual activities, which involved women a generation younger than himself. He had become the seducer instead of the seduced in an endless compulsive repetition in his attempts to get mastery over the trauma. In addition to the sexual abuse, the reverend had been traumatized by his father's disgrace: his fall from minister to sexton. He had received little parenting from his father, who was clinically insane, or from his mother, whose entire emotional life was spent trying to quell the father's outbursts of rage and to provide economically for the family. Unlike his parents, both the man and the woman who seduced him had spent time with him and, despite exploiting him, had made him feel loved and valued. These were feelings that he lacked at home, so "love" for Reverend Smith was sex from a very early age. He had never dealt with the traumatic events of his childhood but instead turned to drugs, alcohol, and sex.

His periodic abstinence from alcohol was not really sobriety because his third addiction—sex, whether acted on or not—was all consuming. Reverend Smith had great contempt for his congregation, whom he described as a bunch of lower-middle-class "boobs," and he constantly attempted to shore up his abysmal self-esteem by being condescending to other people, including the Presbyterian minister and the president of his congregation. He was so openly contemptuous and antagonistic that the renewal of his contract was already in doubt. His stated goal in therapy was to stay sober, and I helped him do that. He also did not act out with the Presbyterian minister, but his repressed emotional pain was so intense and his need to run from it so strong that we really did not get very far in resolving the unconscious determinants of his sexual compulsiveness.

I am not sure what the reverend's religious beliefs were, but, ironically, spirituality did not seem to be his strong suit. He was bitter, filled with rage, and knew how to do only two things with those intolerable feelings: to chemically anesthetize them or to divert his attention from them by obsessing about women. The rush of orgasm was almost incidental—obsessing was almost as good as having sex. Therefore, sexual abstinence, which for him might have meant being faithful to his wife, would not really solve his problem because he already had long periods during which he was technically faithful yet was unable to get away from his obsessive thoughts. Unfortunately, this mental preoccupation never stopped. Reverend Smith was one of the most tormented men I have seen in psychotherapy. He lived in fear, was racked by guilt, and could not really do his job because his mind, almost literally, did not belong to him. It bothers me that I was unable to help him more than I did. What I did was crisis intervention, which was good but not enough. Although it was important for the reverend to stop drinking (because it prevented self-destruction from alcoholism), he needed to go beyond this, to get in touch with and work through the anguish of his traumatic childhood.

Tom's attempts at recovery did not work either. He also had a cross-addiction to drugs and alcohol. My first meeting with Tom was different than most initial sessions. His was the strangest presenting problem that I had ever heard. He said, "I'm here because my wife objects to my putting butter on my penis so our dog will lick it off."

Tom's wife, Susan, had complained to the leaders of their church about her husband's abhorrent behavior, and it had infuriated Tom. He felt that she had no right to speak to his spiritual mentors about his predilections. Tom went on to say that he did not know why his wife was still so upset because the ruling body of his religious sect had ruled that he was not guilty of bestiality because he had not had intercourse with his dog. He was quite triumphant as he told me of the legalistic wrangling that had led to his exoneration and had averted his excommunication.

Similarly, Clinton is said to have used religion to excuse certain behaviors. He reportedly confided in a friend that oral sex must be okay because the Bible does not regard it as adultery. Some commentators have anticipated that Clinton's denial of having sexual relationships with various women, including Monica Lewinsky, will be defended by his assertion that oral sex is somehow different from a *sexual relationship,* a term that would apply only to sexual intercourse. Both arguments are pathetic, weak attempts to justify and rationalize behaviors that both men know to be wrong.

Tom quickly told me that his canine love relationship was not really the problem because he had agreed to cease involving the dog in his sex life. He went on to explain what he saw as the real problem: pornographic videos. I asked him about them, and he said, "Well, the problem really isn't the videos, the problem is that I try not to watch them. In order to do this, I keep the television and VCR under lock and key, and then I try to hide the key from myself." I inquired further. "Yes," he said, "if I can find the key, then I'm going to watch the videos, and then I masturbate for hours at a time. Sometimes I masturbate for days at a time." "And your wife does not object to that?" I asked. "No, what she objects to is the kids not being able to watch television."

I asked him to tell me a little more about himself. Tom told me of his life on the West Coast as a kind of wanderer and of having spent his youth as a sort of hobo working occasionally in the building trades. His nomadic existence was a romantic memory. He remembered dropping acid on mountaintops in the Sierras. As he spoke, my image of him changed from that of a tramp to that of a hippie. Indeed, he had spent his share of time in Haight-Ashbury, had done a lot of acid, and then had discovered methamphetamines (commonly known as speed). He truly loved speed, and I concluded that he must have been a pretty depressed guy to be so strongly attracted to stimulants. Although Tom spoke freely of his recent past, I had a very hard time eliciting any sort of early history. His childhood seemed to be one huge blank. I inferred that it must have been pretty horrible and that he had blocked most of it out. I never did learn much except that his father had been alcoholic and that his mother had died when he was very young. He had been raised by his grandmother, who seemed to be a kindly yet ineffectual "spaced-out" lady.

Although extremely intelligent, Tom had dropped out of high school and drifted into the counterculture. He spent all his 20s sporadically reading poetry, hanging out, playing the guitar, dropping acid, and taking speed. As far as I could tell, he did not have much of any sex life at all, so his sex life ended up being masturbation. Tom ultimately told me that he had been a compulsive masturbater as far back as he could remember, and he had clear memories of rubbing his penis raw as a small boy.

He said that for a long time he was afraid of girls and that he played it safe by playing with himself. He said that he rarely masturbated when he was on acid but that speed and masturbation were strongly linked in his mind. When he was high on methamphetamine, he could fantasize in exciting ways and spend literally days masturbating. Somewhere in his early 30s he had started hitchhiking across the country and wound up in the East, where he met his wife, a member of the religious group to which he now belongs. She, too, had been a counterculture high school dropout and a flaky, disorganized kid from a crazy home, but she had found the Lord. I never did get a coherent account of how these two people met, but I gathered that it was something like love at first sight. Sue had insisted that he give up drugs, and for the most part he did. Although he had dropped acid a few times, he had not used speed for over 10 years.

Using skills that he had picked up during his nomadic years, he got a job and settled down, ultimately becoming a construction manager. He was quite successful economically, and the family lived well. He had built their home, which was large and elaborate, and had risen steadily in the construction trade, performing many functions of an architect or engineer despite not having any formal training in either field. He had a kind of creativity in his line of work that was well respected.

People never cease to amaze me with their areas of function and dysfunction and all the internal contradictions they manifest.

Tom's on-the-job problem was that he would need to run off to find a place to masturbate, which he did at least a dozen times a day. I wondered how this man, now in his 40s, could possibly have such a high libido. His particular addiction was on the verge of psychosis.

Tom and Sue had gotten along fairly well. Because he was not drugging, she had no great objection to his masturbating, and they had a highly active and reportedly mutually satisfying sexual relationship. The problem had started when he got into videos a few years before he came in for treatment. He became progressively more obsessed with the videos, and his masturbation took over more of his life, impoverishing his relationship with his wife and two small children. Sue was also worried that the children would learn what Daddy did for hours at a time. This did not concern her because she objected to sex but because she knew that there was something, as she put it, "odd" about his behavior.

Like Clinton, Tom and Sue's participation in church had stabilized them and allowed them to more or less function. His congregation seemed to regard him highly. Economically, he did better than most of his fellow parishioners, and he faithfully attended the meetings and services of the group. In fact, at one point there was talk of elevating him to a leadership position. I think it was the economic threat that shook Sue somewhat loose from her coaddiction. She was still willing to enable a good deal of sexual addiction, but not the amount that Tom was now displaying. The situation was reminiscent of the codependent who does not object to her husband's drinking per se but does want him to drink "normally" even though he is an alcoholic and incapable of doing this. Sue wanted Tom to masturbate "normally" and to give her the key to the VCR so the children, like the other children in the neighborhood, could watch the programs their peers watched. Tom would not relinquish the keys because he claimed that if he did he would be totally out of control and would masturbate all the time.

Tom's addiction and Sue's coaddiction remained untreated, progressing until his sex addiction was so powerful that the couple's livelihood was in jeopardy. His frequent absences from the work site were drawing increasingly unfavorable attention from the owners of his company.

I doubt that either Sue or Tom dramatized or exaggerated the situation. Sue, who came for several individual and some couples' sessions, had an oddness about her that suggested that she had some secrets that she was not ready to share. She struck me as extremely unrealistic and, in many ways, the more immature of the two. I think the "deal" was that she could remain the little girl, playing house, and he would take care of her as long as she did not say too much about what he did with his penis. The Clintons are also alleged by personal friends and some biographers to have a "deal": Hillary ignores his philanderings and defends him from allegations concerning his sex life in exchange for power or, at least, closeness to power. It is said that Hillary, early on, believed that Bill would be president some day and that she wanted to go along for the ride. Tom and Sue's arrangement "worked" for quite a few years, but by the time Tom came for treatment, it had stopped working. The progression of his addiction had violated the unspoken understanding between them, and she no longer felt compelled to keep her part of the bargain (one wonders if this might happen with Hillary).

Sue had not only complained to the church leaders about Tom's sexual exploitation of their dog but also threatened to call the Humane Society. That shook up Tom. He was off the hook with his church, as his behavior was ruled not to be bestiality, but now he was threatened with the loss of his beloved pet. He did seem to genuinely love the dog; in fact, he spoke even more about the dog than he did about his wife. Clearly, his perception that it was not the bizarreness of his sexual relationship with the dog as much as his wife's jealousy of his relationship with the dog had led to the present crisis. This was a really disturbed couple, and I did not quite know what to do with them. I told Tom about Sexual Compulsives Anonymous, but he would have no part of it. His resistance took the form of saying that his spiritual needs were met by his church and that to go elsewhere would be an act of disloyalty. I replied that trying to get help for sexual addiction from his church was like trying to get his shoes soled at the dry cleaners. The dry cleaner did a terrific job cleaning his clothes but was not specialized to fix shoes. Similarly, his church did a terrific job providing spiritual sustenance to its members but was not specialized to deal with addictions. This is an argument I have used successfully with members of fundamentalist groups who feared that going to 12-step meetings was somehow being disloyal to their religions. Although it has worked in other cases, this would not be the case with Tom.

Unfortunately, the therapy did not progress very far. However, one thing that became clear was that masturbation was an antianxiety drug for Tom. He related that when he had curtailed the masturbation, he had become highly anxious. In fact, he had become so anxious that he had had difficulty doing his job. I wondered how much of that anxiety was a withdrawal symptom because, as you might recall, sex addiction, like all other addictions, does have withdrawal symptoms. But the more I knew Tom, the more clear it became that he had a lifelong problem with anxiety, which he had self-medicated in many different ways. I think the therapy was getting too close to home as we began to probe for the meaning and sources of his anxiety. One day he called me to say that he was doing much better and had been able to give Sue the keys to the VCR and so would not be attending therapy anymore. My efforts to re-engage him failed.

Although he had given up drugs, Tom was what the 12-step programs would call "dry" rather than "sober." This meant that, although he was not using substances, he had not experienced any emotional or spiritual growth, which is an important part of sobriety. In fact, Tom had not taken very many steps toward growth at all. He had been able to marry, establish a career, and gain something from his membership in the church. Part of the problem was that Tom seemed to take much more from the church than he gave to it, and he really needed to give more.

Like many addicts, Tom felt that he would literally die if he stopped his addictive behavior. He and I were unable to overcome the intensity of his fear and anxiety because he fled from the treatment. It was opening up too many issues, including the danger of remembering the traumatic childhood that he had blocked out for so long. I think the real problem was that outpatient psychotherapy was not sufficient for him. If he had been willing to enter an inpatient rehabilitation unit, I think his chances of recovery would have been good. An extended inpatient experience would have given him the opportunity to work on himself without being distracted or feeling the pressures of family and professional life. It would also have provided a "holding environment." Because he would have been unable to "act out," he would have had no choice but to "act in": to look within himself and come to terms with the demons driving his compulsion.

Unlike Reverend Smith and Tom, and despite all the complications and difficulties of rehabilitating from a sexual addiction, it has been shown that people can and do recover. So, what makes recovery easier? An early diagnosis of the problem. Consider breast cancer. Cancer is a progressive disease, so the earlier a diagnosis is made, the better the chances are for recovery. The same logic applies to addictions. I have illustrated the progressive nature of addictions and shown how they eventually take over the addict's entire life. Just like cancer, the earlier a diagnosis is made, the better the chances are for recovery.

Having a strong support system helps as well. Although friends and families can offer support and encouragement, they can also enable one's addiction and thereby undermine one's efforts at recovery. Therefore, it often is necessary for the sex addict to find a new support system. For many people, that support system turns out to be a 12-step program.

CHAPTER EIGHT

Step by Step

ALCOHOLICS ANONYMOUS (A.A.) was the first of the 12-step programs. It is a fellowship of men and women whose purpose is to stop drinking. It holds meetings all over the world that are open to anyone, no questions asked.

A.A. is a unique organization. It has changed millions of lives and has served as a model for numerous other self-help groups. It was started in the 1930s by Bill Wilson, an alcoholic stockbroker, and Bob Smith, an alcoholic physician. Bill was not in any shape to sell stocks, so he could not have caused you any difficulty; but Bob Smith was a practicing Akron, Ohio, surgeon specializing in proctology. If you had hemorrhoids in Akron in the 1930s, you were in trouble. Bill W., as he is known in A.A. (members are identified by first name and last initial only to protect their anonymity), had a "peak experience," an intensely emotional affirmation of the worthwhileness of life, while he was a patient drying out in Knickerbocker Hospital. Bill was shaken to his core by his experience in Knickerbocker. He went through a profound emotional reorganization and left the hospital as a different person. The religiously inclined interpret Bill's emotional revelation as a "conversion experience." The more secularly inclined interpret it as a reaction to his insight that his despair was caused by his drinking and need not continue. In any case, Bill's peak experience gave him hope and served as his bottom.

Bill entered Knickerbocker after talking to his drinking buddy, Ebby Thacker, who one day showed up at Bill's place a changed man. Bill poured himself a drink, and as he drank it, Ebby told Bill of joining the Oxford Group, which was an upper-class revival movement that had its origins at Oxford University. It aimed at converting the leading men in a community with the hope that their example would spread down the ranks. Ebby told Bill that he had been sober since joining, and he recommended that Bill join as well. Wilson did so when he left Knickerbocker. He stayed sober, but he was not comfortable with the Oxford movement's dogmatism. On a business trip to Akron, Bill found himself tormented by a desire to drink. However, he had the insight that he would not act on his desire if he could find another alcoholic to help in the way that Ebby had helped him. Bill found Bob Smith, who was too shaky to perform a scheduled operation. Bill fed Bob a beer on his way to surgery, stopping Bob's shakes. As they drove, Bill told Bob his story. In that act of sharing both the torments of drinking and the joys of recovery, A.A. was born. Neither man ever drank again. They had discovered that something is special, even curative, about two people with the same problem sharing their "experience, strength, and hope." Bill soon discovered that open sharing and identification helps problem drinkers regardless of their personalities or circumstances. It still does. It changes the way they feel about themselves, it changes their drinking, and it changes their lives.

Returning to New York, Bill left the Oxford Group, organized meetings for alcoholics, and founded A.A. The Oxford Movement recommended a series of steps for spiritual growth to its members. Bill modified them into A.A.'s 12 Steps of Recovery. A.A. grew rapidly and today is a worldwide organization with a vast membership. It works very well for many, but not all, people with drinking problems. Nevertheless, it is the best single bet for achieving comfortable, enjoyable sobriety.

One of the most curative elements of A.A. is acceptance. The people who have come for help have been reviled, criticized, and put down by family, friends, employers, law enforcement officers, and so on. All that hatred has been internalized, and they hate themselves as well. Being accepted by the fellowship gives people the chance to begin to love themselves. It sounds hokey, but it works as long as they continue to attend meetings and are able to open up emotionally to the warmth and friendship available. The sharing that occurs at its meetings is what makes recovery in A.A. such a unique experience.

What is an A.A. meeting like? The two types of meetings are open and closed. Open meetings are open to anyone. I send my students to these. At an open meeting, the chairperson (a rotating office) reads the A.A. preamble and introduces the speaker, who "qualifies" (tells his or her story). A.A. qualifications consist of a "drunk-a-log," which is an account of the speaker's experience with alcohol and an account of what sobriety has been like for that person. After the qualifications, the chairperson closes the meeting with the A.A. Serenity Prayer: "God grant me the serenity to accept the things I cannot change, courage to change the things I can, and wisdom to know the difference." There is no discussion, and the "audience" does not participate, so there is absolutely no pressure of any kind on those who attend open A.A. meetings. At most meetings, participants get coffee and cookies. At some point, a basket is passed into which one can place no more than a dollar but is not required to do so.

Closed meetings are restricted to "those who have a desire to stop drinking." Usually, a speaker's qualification is followed by discussion, which is sometimes structured by going around the room, person to person. But you do not have to say anything; you can just say, "I pass," and no one will press you. A.A. is nonconfrontational. I strongly urge you to go to an A.A. meeting. It is a fascinating experience. The openness and honesty manifested at most A.A. meetings touch people at a deep level regardless of whether they have a drinking problem. Of course, like any group of people, A.A. has its losers—members who are obnoxious, unlikable, or downright mean. As they say in A.A., "principles before personalities," so a potential member should not let a speaker whom he or she dislikes or a member who rubs them the wrong way discourage them or turn them off. The trick is to identify, not compare. Being overly critical and feeling different from the others at the meeting are in the service of denial—it's the disease telling people that they do not have it. One need not like everything about A.A. to benefit from it.

A.A. meetings reflect their communities. A meeting in a village in Vermont will be somewhat different from a meeting in Greenwich Village, yet it will be the same. People who are concerned about anonymity can go to A.A. meetings outside their community, but they should go where they are likely to feel comfortable. In my experience, A.A. has an excellent record keeping memberships private and in preserving the anonymity of members. New members are urged to get "sponsors," which are A.A. members of stable sobriety who act as mentors.

In addition to meetings, A.A. offers a 12-step program that leads to spiritual or emotional growth. This program has been so successful in helping individuals recover from the addiction of alcohol that it has been adopted by other recovery groups.

Today, 12-step fellowships exist for most recognized addictions: for alcohol, Alcoholics Anonymous (A.A.); for overeaters, Overeaters Anonymous (O.A.); for drug users, Narcotics Anonymous (N.A.); and for gamblers, Gamblers Anonymous (G.A.). For sexual addiction, there are a number of competing groups: Sexaholics Anonymous (S.A.), Sexual Compulsives Anonymous (S.C.A.), Sex Addicts Anonymous (S.A.A.), and Sex and Love Addicts Anonymous (S.L.A.A.).

Most of these groups work similarly to A.A. The addict attends meetings, shares and listens, tries to identify with speakers, forms an alliance with a sponsor, and works the 12 steps.

The 12-step programs speak of the necessity of "hitting bottom." One is said to have hit bottom when he or she experiences the lowest point imaginable in his or her life and actually faces the deepest pain associated with addiction. This experience leads not only to despair but also to a "surrender" that comes in the form of an admission that one is powerless over alcohol, sex, gambling, cocaine, and so on. This surrender is, in essence, the first step in recovery.

The first step states, "We admit to ourselves that we are powerless over our sexual compulsion and that our compulsion made our lives unmanageable." This is the step that deals with denial. It is a Zen paradox in that by admitting one's powerlessness one becomes empowered. By relinquishing denial, it is possible not only to begin to change one's behavior but also to change one's entire emotional and interpersonal life. It is no longer necessary to be dishonest with other people, so one is no longer caught up in a tangled web of lies, pretenses, rationalizations, and excuses.

David was on a pass from a "rehab" when he hit bottom and relinquished his denial. It happened at an A.A. meeting, and he described it as follows:

The meeting started. The preamble was read: "Alcoholics Anonymous is a fellowship of men and women who share their experience, strength, and hope with each other. . . ." Something happened. Those words sounded like pure poetry.

The speaker was a beautiful young woman, intensely and vibrantly alive. Her vivacity and sparkle certainly facilitated what was about to happen. She spoke of her years of drugging and drinking, of her progressive spiritual and emotional death. Finally, she said, "I got to the point that I couldn't feel anything. For no particular reason I went on a trip across the country with some drinking buddies. As we crossed the country, my feelings became more and more frozen. We arrived at the Grand Canyon. I looked at it and felt nothing. I knew that I should be responding with awe and wonder to the sight before me, but I couldn't. I had always loved nature, now that love, like everything else about me, was dead. I decided to take a picture of the magnificence spread before me so that if I ever unmelted I could look at the picture and feel what I couldn't feel then."

At that moment, something incredible happened to me. I completely identified with the speaker, and in that identification I hit bottom. I knew then that I couldn't continue drinking and live. I understood her frozen feelings; they were mine. I understood her wish to preserve a precious moment in the hope that someday she could adequately respond with feelings of awe and wonder to it. Something welled up in me. I began to sob, deep, strong, powerful sobs; they did not stop for the hour and a half that the meeting lasted. As the speaker told her story—how she managed to stop drugging and drinking and how her feelings had become unfrozen—my feelings became unfrozen. I was still crying when I shook her hand and thanked her. I walked out of the meeting feeling happy. Happy, Doctor. I couldn't ever remember feeling happy.

As I walked down the street toward the hospital, the tears were still flowing. Now they were tears of happiness and gratitude. I, who had been so formal and controlled and concerned to impress, walked past staring strollers with tears streaming down completely indifferent to, indeed oblivious of, their reactions. Doctor, do you know Edna St. Vincent Millay's poem "Renascence"? It tells of a young women who has been buried, then the rain comes washing her grave away, returning her to life. She becomes aware of "A fragrance such as never clings/To aught save happy living things. . . ." I had always loved that poem; now I truly understood it. My tears were like the rain in the poem; they, like the rain, washed me out of the grave I had dug for myself with alcohol and emotional repression. I too smelled the fragrance that never clings to aught save happy living things.

Once denial breaks down and the first step is accepted (the addiction is arrested), recovering people are destined to eventually start liking themselves because, one day at a time, they regain control of their lives, and that newfound power feels good. They are no longer dominated by their addictions, and they come to realize that the only person they *need* to control, and the only person they *can* control, is themselves. Self-esteem begins to rise, and the need for external confirmation of their worth becomes much less important until eventually there is no need to be a people-pleaser after all.

The second step states, "We believe that a power greater than ourselves can restore us to sanity." This step does two things: It emphasizes the insanity of the addiction, thus breaking down denial and leading to insight, and it provides hope by affirming that there is a distinct, higher power that is available to the individual to assist recovery. This higher power can be thought of as the forces within oneself (which create growth or healing), as a kind of transcendental religious figure (such as God), or as the A.A. group itself. The important notion is that such a power *exists* regardless of its form and that it can restore the alcoholic's sanity.

The third step states, "We turn our will and our lives over to God as we understand him." This, the most explicitly religious of the steps, turns many people off. I often secularize it for people by rephrasing it as, "Let it happen." The 12-step slogan, "Get out of the driver's seat," says pretty much the same thing. This step is about relinquishing control and going with the flow. It opens people up to get better and to recover without resistance. We have already seen how addictions are very much about trying to control the uncontrollable, about controlling not only the self but others as well. We have seen how sex addicts try to control other people because they lack control over other areas of their lives.

The third step works in yet another way. By relinquishing control and turning over one's life to one's "God," the addict relieves a lot of anxiety, much of which has helped feed the addictive behavior in the past. Recall that addictions help individuals self-medicate their own anxiety. Once this anxiety is gone, less need for "medication" exists. It is very difficult for addicts to relinquish control because we all must keep *some* control over our lives. The idea here is to put in the effort and then let go—do what you can but realize that, one way or another, you are going to be all right regardless of the outcome.

No one turns his or her will over once and for all. It is a kind of undulating lifelong process. The aim is to gain awareness of maladaptive and pathological attempts to control oneself and others and try to stop this behavior when it happens.

The fourth step talks about making a "fearless moral inventory of ourselves." Here, *fearless* refers to being utterly honest in making one's list, knowing that there is nothing to be afraid of. Recovering addicts fear their own judgments of themselves the most (their consciences) and, to a lesser extent, the judgments of others. The projection of self-blame can give these fears a tinge of paranoia. My experience with recovering addicts of all kinds is that they get hung up on the fourth step because of these fears.

Bill Wilson, the founder of A.A., recommends dividing the list into assets and liabilities, almost like an accounting balance sheet. This helps the addict gain a more realistic picture of who he or she is. Wilson sagely commented, "The more depressive among us will see no assets, while the high rollers will see no deficits." This is the same notion as optimistic people seeing the proverbial glass as "half full" and pessimistic people seeing it as "half empty."

The purpose of the inventory is not to make people feel more guilty about having been addicts or having done the self-centered, sometimes cruel, or even criminal things that people do to maintain their addictions. Rather, the purpose is to alleviate guilt and shame. My experience is that working the fourth step is extraordinarily liberating. People leave a lot of garbage behind when they do this step well because making such a list helps them face reality and take responsibility for their lives. This ability to face reality, as awful as that reality might be, raises self-esteem and leads to an acceptance of the finality of the past and the realization that today can be better.

The fifth step recommends that the recovering person "share" the fourth step with another person. It states, "We admit to ourselves, to another person, and to God the exact nature of our wrongs." Confession as a vehicle of personal growth has been a part of all religious traditions and all psychotherapies because individuals inevitably feel greatly relieved to finally share their long-hidden guilt.

I knew a recovering addict who had difficulty with the "admitting to God" part because he was an atheist. He worked around this by driving to the ocean and reading his list out loud, thereby sharing it with the sea instead.

The sixth and seventh steps concern willingness to change; the eighth and ninth steps concern making amends to people whom the addict has hurt (but only if doing so would not hurt further); the tenth step recommends taking a daily moral inventory; the eleventh step speaks about increasing one's conscious contact with God through prayer and meditation (a turnoff for many people); and the twelfth step talks about having a spiritual awakening as a result of working the steps and making a decision to practice these principles in all of one's affairs. The corollary to this is to try to help other people recover. To "12-step" someone is to tell one's story to an active addict in the hope that he or she will identify with one's story and move toward recovery.

The movement also advises its participants to make no major changes during the first year of recovery. On the surface, the purpose of this advice is to avoid having the individual make decisions while in withdrawal. During withdrawal, the individual is on shaky ground and is not likely to make good decisions. This advice is given for another reason as well. Those with experience in the 12-step movement know that the first-year recovering addict is not strong enough to bear the unconscious terror that accompanies the dizziness of freedom. Being faced early in recovery with this dizziness of freedom can lead to relapse because the addict might seek to flee again from the newfound responsibility.

I recommend that sex addicts at least try the 12-step program. I tell my patients that they need not buy the whole thing lock, stock, and barrel but that they can view it as a smorgasbord and take what they can use. The reality is that people use the 12-step programs in all kinds of ways and do well. I have known people who have become deeply and emotionally involved with their program and have worked long and hard on the steps. I have also known people who have done very well by doing little or nothing with the steps beyond using them as a support system. Let me clearly state that *joining a 12-step group is not the only way to recover from an addiction.*

The 12-step program (used in conjunction with private, individual therapy) worked for Jack, a strikingly handsome homosexual man who was involved in the entertainment business. He sang, danced, and acted both on stage and in nightclubs. He would cruise compulsively, sometimes having as many as 30 partners in a 24-hour period. Although his preference was to have another man go down on him, he engaged in every possible sexual act in both the passive and the active position. Although he made sporadic attempts to protect himself, he often engaged in unsafe sex.

Sex dominated Jack's life. He risked not only his health but also getting arrested by having sex during the day in public places such as parks. Although he worked diligently at his art and craft, most of the time he was thinking about sex. Undoubtedly, Jack received pleasure from his sexual activities, but the pleasure played a relatively small part in scoring. Jack was not seeking the physical pleasure as much as the reassurance that he was desirable. Each time he engaged in sex, however, the reassurance did not last for more than a few minutes, so yet another partner was necessary to give him the momentary illusion that he was lovable.

It was almost as if he would shatter if he could not have sex. He was afraid of "going to pieces" or of "falling apart" unless he was wanted by someone. This kind of falling apart is what psychologists call *fragmenting,* and his fear of it made his life a living hell. What if he did not score? What if he did not find a sufficient number of partners? The anxiety that the mere thought engendered in Jack was more than he could stand. Jack also had a long history of cross-addiction to alcohol and cocaine, and although he was actively engaged in both Alcoholics Anonymous and Narcotics Anonymous, he had never dealt with his equally destructive sexual addiction.

His history was fascinating. His mother dominated everything. Having artistic talent, she made a living selling designs to architects and doing various jobs in the decorating business. She was also extremely active in politics and had been involved as a campaign manager in her community during John F. Kennedy's run for president. She even knew Kennedy personally. Jack was only a young child when Kennedy was assassinated. Following the assassination, his mother began calling him "my John-John." She had photographs of Kennedy all over the house, and Jack even looked strikingly like John Kennedy. As an adult, he became convinced that he was John Kennedy's illegitimate son.

Like Clinton's stepfather, Jack's father had never done very well in life. He had difficulty holding jobs and had done little parenting. He was in the advanced stages of alcoholism by the time his wife left him, although he eventually settled down to a kind of maintenance drinking.

When Jack came in for therapy, he complained of depression and difficulty functioning on a daily basis. He did not readily see his sex life as a problem, although that knowledge was not too far beneath the surface. N.A. had broken down his denial of his sexual addiction but not far enough to overcome his rationalizations of his behavior. In the course of therapy, a therapy in which I repeatedly made a connection between his sexual behavior and his difficulties in functioning, his denial slowly but steadily eroded. We talked about all the issues in his life that had pushed him to develop a sexual addiction. During therapy, Jack not only talked but *felt* as well, especially the shame of having an alcoholic father. He also came into contact with how erotic and seductive his mother had been with him and how he turned the passive into the active and attempted to master the trauma of childhood sexual abuse by becoming an addict.

Finally, Jack told me one day that he had joined Sexual Compulsives Anonymous, where he felt at home. He felt understood, and he came to accept that sex was just as much an addiction as alcohol and cocaine had been for him in the past. In S.C.A. Jack found other sexual compulsives with whom he could identify. By sharing his own story, he was able to reduce his guilt and shame. The other members of his group gave him practical suggestions that he could use to deal with his "urges." In S.C.A. they talked about sex (not drugs), and Jack, although familiar with the 12 steps, needed the specificity of S.C.A. to help him gain control of his compulsion.

S.C.A. did not lead to immediate behavioral changes, but over the course of time it eventually did. Jack worked out an abstinence plan that demanded not complete abstinence from sex but simply an attempt at being less impulsive and compulsive and generally more in control. He relapsed from time to time, but the relapses became increasingly less frequent. He now saw his problem as finding a partner to whom he could commit. Eventually, he did fall in love with a man, but his lover did not treat him well, and the relationship ended in a way that was excruciatingly painful for Jack. I expected him to relapse and to turn as many tricks as he could. He talked about it but did not act on it.

Jack had grown a great deal in learning how to experience the pains of rejection rather than anesthetizing them. He now had far more energy to pursue his artistic goals, and his career took off. In the past, poverty had been a major source of pain in his life, and it had given him a rationalization for cruising in that it brought temporary pleasure but cost him nothing financially. Now that his career was booming, his economic position improved, and his self-esteem rose. Jack is a success story, having benefited from both therapy and S.C.A.

Sandy also used S.C.A. with individual therapy sessions to overcome her addiction. Initially, she came to therapy because of a work problem. An editor for a top-drawer magazine, she had graduated from an Ivy League college with honors but had been in the same entry-level job for five years. She was frustrated and bitter when she came for treatment. She alternated between railing at her employer and the politics of the magazine for which she worked and blaming herself for not working up to her potential. From what she told me, I never would have known that she had a sex life (addictive or otherwise). All she talked about was how unhappy she was at her job and how disappointed she was that her job did not allow her to work up to her potential. Finally, she started talking about what she did after work.

Sandy made the "singles scene," although, unlike many sex addicts, she was not much of a drinker or a drug user. Since coming to the city, she had had a succession of short-term affairs and had not been faithful to any of her partners. After work, she would go back to her apartment, in tears over her frustration at still doing a routine clerical job that offered only the occasional chance to edit. Then she would hurry out to one of the singles bars in her neighborhood. It was a rare night that she did not wind up in bed with someone, often with a man for whom she simply did not care. She would be somewhat puzzled about that but would rationalize it by saying, "There are no bad orgasms." She had no idea that she had a problem with sexual behavior, not even when she became infected with genital herpes.

Despite all her brilliance, Sandy worked on the surface and could not go deep, whether editing a manuscript or being in a relationship. She stayed on the surface for powerful reasons. Any form of engagement or commitment was terrifying to her because her father had been killed in a car accident when she was quite young (four years old), and her mother, who quickly remarried, had emotionally abandoned her. Like Bill Clinton, she had not been overtly abused in any way, but she had been left to her own devices and received a minimum of biologically necessary care. For these reasons, she was unable to get close to anyone, and she had soothed herself through masturbation from an early age.

Sometimes she overheard her mother and stepfather's lovemaking, and, because she had a vague notion of what they were doing, it excited her. She became a compulsive masturbater, and this became her way of self-soothing. It provided her with some kind of satisfaction and reassurance, and it was the one thing she knew she could always rely on.

Her high level of intelligence allowed her to sail through school, and she won numerous honors, but her mother and stepfather paid little attention to her achievements. In fact, they did not even show up for the award ceremony held during her senior year. She went off to an Ivy League college as a virgin and quickly discovered casual sex, which made her feel in control because she did not stay with anyone long enough to let them abandon her. She continued to rationalize her behavior by viewing sex as a natural high. She was really a very sad and pathetic young woman.

As an adult, Sandy was out of control, but she did not know it. She could no more go home after work and think about editing a manuscript than she could fly to the moon. Instead, she had to go to a singles bar, find a partner (or partners) who would assure her that she was lovable and loved, and then leave him. This abandoning was a reenactment of her mother's abandoning her for a man. In this way she felt safe, but her life was impoverished.

My first job as therapist was to drive in a wedge and help Sandy see that the way she was living was problematic. I focused on the herpes and some other physical problems she was having. Slowly, she began to recognize that her behavior was indeed a problem. Her denial was becoming porous, and although it was a long, slow process, Sandy eventually gained some insight into what she was doing and why she was doing it. This did not lead to an immediate behavioral change, but I had not expected it to.

One of the most curative elements in her therapy was her relationship with me. Over a period of several years, she came to trust me, and it was the first trusting relationship in her life since her father's sudden, traumatic death. Only after feeling safe in therapy did she slowly acquire the courage to risk feeling connected to a man for whom she had romantic and erotic feelings. However, she was unable to be faithful to him as well, and she lost him. She was devastated. The pain of this loss was her bottom. For the first time, she saw and felt that her sexual compulsion was ruining her life.

It took several more years of therapy to solidify her gains. She joined a 12-step group (S.C.A.) and became involved in a committed but stormy relationship. Once she realized that the pain of nonrecognition at her job had recapitulated the pain of nonrecognition at home, she left her employment and took a job in a completely different field. She now works in a far less cerebral field, but one in which she receives recognition, and she is now able to use her considerable intellectual talent.

In my practice, I have found a 12-step group that is not directed at sex addicts but which is, nevertheless, extremely helpful for many them: Adult Children of Alcoholics (ACOA). ACOA is beneficial for sex addicts because most of them come from alcoholic or otherwise dysfunctional homes. ACOA is effective in getting people to deal with the effects of growing up in such homes, which in turn can make recovery from their own addiction much easier. Like Sandy, Ted was also helped by joining a 12-step fellowship.

Ted was a gay man who, from time to time, was episodically out of control sexually. He was a handsome, bright, and witty musician who came into therapy with a cross-addiction to drinking. He came to terms with his alcoholism rather early in therapy and spent a number of years as an enthusiastic A.A. member, slowly pulling away from the program, as many do. He had little or no difficulty putting the cork in the bottle and achieving sobriety. He did not like what alcohol was doing to him, as it exacerbated his depression. In his younger years, he was inhibited and somewhat sexually repressed, so he used alcohol to loosen up so that he could cruise. Now, after a couple years of therapy and some life experience, he had little difficulty being sexual while sober, and he did not need to drink to pick up men. Although Ted had a clear awareness of sexual addiction, he disidentified with it; that is, he would talk about other gay men being sexually compulsive but felt that he was not. Ted's problem with sex happened only when he was feeling hurt or shamed. When he experienced what psychiatrists call a *narcissistic wound* (a deep, lacerating blow to one's self-esteem), he reacted first with shame at having been treated that way and then with rage. It might surprise you to learn that shame is a reaction to being mistreated. We are ashamed of being treated like dirt, and we do not want anyone to know that we have been treated that way. This is especially true of maltreatment in childhood. Children who have been physically and sexually abused are dominated by shame, as are children of alcoholics (such as Bill Clinton). Eventually, the shame reaches the point at which it becomes the individual's controlling emotion. In a less intense way, shame is an inevitable consequence of life's blows. People are ashamed of having addictions, of having cancer, of being fired, of being out of control, of having been rejected, and of having their work ridiculed.

Ted's shame and rage came mostly from his work being ridiculed. He was an avant-garde composer and a performer of spectacular dexterity. His work was controversial and often ridiculed—not only by other musicians and the critics but sometimes by his family as well. His mother would say things such as, "Why don't you write some popular stuff and make a few bucks?" "Who do you think you are, Schoenberg?" "You're trying to do things that are over your head. Try something easier."

In an effort to be supportive, I conceded to attend a concert of Ted's. His music sounded like noise to me, which put me in a terrible bind. I have always made a point of being honest with patients. It is so important that patients are treated directly and with respect, so although I always try to be tactful, I never (if I can help it) say anything that I do not believe to be true. Still, I simply could not tell Ted that I thought his work was just plain awful, so I convinced myself that I was simply uncultured in the area of avant-garde music. I told myself that this was probably great stuff and that, because some people really do like his music, this problem was mine, not his.

Only then was I was able to say that I was surprised at the originality of his work, having never heard anything like it before (which was true), and that it was something that I needed to savor to appreciate (also true). He did not push me for any further response, and I believe that my positive words helped counter the negatives ones from his family.

In fact, it was his family's and his peers' devaluing and humiliating comments that would cause Ted to act out sexually, and, when he did, it was always in an extremely self-destructive way. He would react to the critical scorn, neglect, and disapproving comments by his musical peers by heading for the bathhouses and having sex for days on end with as many people as he possibly could. He was a binge sexual addict, and his binges always were *rage reactions*. Rage fuels many addictions, including sexual ones.

Ted's acting-out episodes were not only rage reactions but also attempts to shore up his extremely fragile self-esteem, which had been shattered by mother, father, friend, and critic. His only way of proving that he was worth anything was to have many men want to have sex with him.

He obsessed about the size of his penis, which he considered small, and felt adequate as a man only when other men wanted to have oral sex with him. When he hit the baths or other cruising spots, he always looked to be the dominant partner. When he was hurt the deepest, he would find a man who wanted to be a passive partner in anal intercourse and would not use a condom in the act. This is certainly a mad act in these days of HIV infection and AIDS. Mad as it was, it served a powerful psychodynamic function, being the ultimate expression of both his rage and his need for self-destruction. He certainly got sensual pleasure out of his sexual encounters, even though they were not about sex; rather, they were about desperate attempts to cement the fragments of a shattered self.

Ted's fragility was a direct result of a childhood that had been extraordinarily traumatic and had predisposed him to narcissistic injury in adulthood. In his own way, he suffered from posttraumatic stress disorder and had adapted to dealing with all that damage by becoming an artist. When his art was rejected or ridiculed, especially by his family members, the traumas of his childhood were repeated, and he was shattered, just as he had been shattered in his childhood. He then tried to turn it around and humiliate and shame someone else by dominating them sexually. He was turning the passive into the active. His anal intercourse with other men had nothing to do with love—it was pure aggression—and because he felt guilty about that aggression, he punished himself by exposing himself to a fatal disease.

After one of these episodic orgies, Ted vowed never to repeat such behavior. He restrained himself by going to the opposite extreme of having no sex life at all for a period of months in an attempt to atone and to stave off the feared punishment of HIV infection. Finally, in fear and trembling, he went for an AIDS test, which proved negative, and he once again vowed never to willingly expose himself to death. Of course, his vow did not last. Another critic would condemn his work or his mother or father would again tell him that he was no genius (and that he should be realistic), and he would be off and running again.

For a long time, my therapeutic goal in working with Ted was not to stop his rageful semirapes of men but simply to get him to use a condom when he engaged in that behavior. Although he never followed my suggestion, this story does have a happy ending. Ted lucked out by never contracting HIV, and eventually he formed a monogamous relationship with a fellow musician who believed that Ted was one of the more important composers of his generation. Now with a loved and loving partner affirming his worth, Ted could survive the blows of hostile criticism without sexually compulsing and self-destructing. Therapy played a large role in Ted's recovery. As he gained insight into what he was doing, he did it less and less. Gradually, he learned to distance himself from his hypercritical and rejecting family and to express his anger at them directly. He also began gaining some recognition in the esoteric world of 12-tone music, and that reassured and stabilized him as well. Ted is a success story. He gained control over his suicidal sexual behavior.

Each of these case histories illustrates that sexual addiction, like all addictions, fails to meet the addicts' increasing emotional needs, and ultimately these needs drive the addict into dangerous, irrational, self-destructive behavior. Not only do addictions fail to fill the inner emptiness, provide reassurance, and quell anxiety, depression, guilt, rage, and shame—they exacerbate each and every one of these symptoms and self-deficits.

Treatment leading to recovery does the opposite—it alleviates the symptoms and ameliorates the self-deficits. Treatment doesn't just patch over the problems, it truly cures.

In this chapter, I have focused on 12-step approaches to recovering from addiction. These approaches work extremely well for many individuals, but they aren't useful to everyone. The following chapter focuses on other therapeutic approaches to recovery that have also been shown to work.

CHAPTER NINE

Beyond the 12 Steps

ALTHOUGH THE 12-STEP PROGRAM works for some people, others find it unacceptable for a variety of reasons, including its public nature. Ask any member of a 12-step program, and they will tell you that the anonymity and confidentiality of meetings is less than perfect. This certainly keeps some people away. Others object to the ideology of these programs not as a resistance to, or in defense of, their addiction but out of a genuine clash of values. They are simply uncomfortable with the spirituality (which many interpret as religiosity) of the program. Some people do not like the 12-step program because it recommends an admission of powerlessness and a realization that the recovery is not brought about by the use of willpower. These individuals believe that their recovery will be more successful if they use willpower, so the notion of powerlessness does not work for them.

Therefore, what is left for individuals who do not want to join a 12-step program? Private (outpatient) individual therapy, private (outpatient) therapy groups, and inpatient programs have proven to be extremely effective. A small number of people have even recovered spontaneously or gained adequate insight simply from reading self-help books. Many of the non-12-step approaches to recovering from addiction are based on the teachings of the psychologist Gordon Marlatt, who created a program he calls *relapse prevention*. It seeks to teach self-efficacy and to help people identify triggers for their addictive behavior.

People with addictions need to learn that both internal and external events can set off their addictive behavior. Once one learns to recognize these events, called *triggers,* one can learn to deal with them in ways other than engaging in the addictive behavior. Identifying triggers prevents relapses but rarely arrests an active addiction. Rather, the addict must first stop the addictive behavior and then learn what his or her triggers are. The triggers are always states of mind and feeling and are usually caused by something external. Feelings of disappointment, sadness, anger, shame, guilt, and low self-esteem are common triggers. For example, if a sexual addict recognizes that one of his triggers is "disappointment," the next time he experiences that emotion he can call a friend or a counselor and discuss both the emotion and the urge instead of engaging in sexual activity. Talking about the urge usually dissipates the compulsive quality of the thought to the point that the addict no longer feels that it is necessary to actually follow through with the behavior.

Some psychologists regard addictions of all kinds (including sexual addiction) as symptoms of an underlying personality disorder. These psychologists work somewhat differently, using a bottom-up approach by trying to help patients get in contact with the unconscious determinants of their addictions in the hope that they will gain control of their behavior through self-knowledge.

The following case history strongly parallels the history of Bill Clinton. It also illustrates the success of one who used private individual therapy and a bottom-up approach to recover.

John was born in a small town in New England, the son of the town drunk. His earliest experiences were of shame and humiliation about his father's drunken behavior. His mother was the responsible, stable, caring parent, but she never left her husband. She made excuses for him, supported him, and made it impossible for her son to acknowledge the pain that he felt seeing his father stumble down the street past his friends. Mother was not overtly seductive, but clearly she put John in the husband role. Therefore, like Clinton, he became a hero early. Mother was all duty and uprightness with little warmth or connection. Bright and charming, John excelled in school from the earliest grades on. He had found a substitute father in the local minister and had planned to become a clergyman himself. Then his plans were derailed.

His repressed anger emerged in the form of rage and eventually got the better of him. During the summer following high school graduation, he became seriously delinquent. Involved in a series of breaking-and-enterings, he was bewildered by his own behavior—it made no sense to him. Like all heroes, he lacked even the slightest awareness that his actions were attempts to regain what he had missed—what he had been cheated of—as a child of an alcoholic.

When he was arrested, he remained in the local jail for several months. He told me that he did not mind being there because "the cooking was so good." I interpreted this as more evidence that his childhood lacked nurturing both at home and from his mother. When he went to trial, a compassionate judge, seeing him as an emotionally troubled youth rather than a criminal, arranged for him to go to college on a scholarship while on probation. Jail turned out to be his "Rhodes scholarship."

John was a virgin when he went to college—but not for long. He had not realized how attractive he was to women, but he quickly discovered that he would have little difficulty finding sexual partners and that sex was one thing that made him feel really good. He discovered that alcohol made him feel good as well, and although he had vowed never to be like his father, he found that he drank more and more as his college years went on. Before he knew it, he was experiencing blackouts—periods that he could not remember—and felt frighteningly out of control. Alcohol raised his self-esteem and gave him a feeling of euphoria—the exact opposite to depression, which was never far from the surface. His fear of becoming like his father resulted in vigorous attempts to control his drinking, which he was able to do by turning more and more to sex. With sex came no hangovers and an endless supply of women.

Unlike most addicts, John knew that he was always on the verge of depression. The sex made him feel loved and lovable, and it moved him even further from his rage and pain than the alcohol ever did. John had a few short-lived relationships that frightened him, so he went back to interchangeable partners. On graduating, he landed a job with a major corporation and climbed the ladder rapidly.

He moved to a big city, where even more women were to be had. For reasons that he himself did not understand, he married one of them. He was unfaithful to her even on their honeymoon night, when he picked someone up in the bar of the hotel in which he and his bride were staying. He had sex with the stranger in the hallway of the hotel and then returned to his room to consummate his marriage. He told me that he felt guilt over the fact that he did not feel guilty. His first marriage did not last long, and two others followed. He was married to his third wife when he came to me for treatment.

John came to me initially because he had recently returned to drinking, which once again had caused a problem—he had received a D.W.I. (driving-while-intoxicated) citation. Fortunately, his renewed problems with alcohol were resolved rather easily because the D.W.I. had really shaken him up. Early in therapy, he put the cork in the bottle, and it stayed there. With his alcohol addiction behind him, John still had a problem to address—his cross-addiction to sex.

John claimed to love his wife, and he rationalized his infidelities as meaningless diversions, though they were not—they were all consuming. John spent hours in his office placing phone calls to lovers, plotting assignations, and arranging his schedule in such a way that work did not interfere with what he jokingly called "his hobby." His current specialty was actresses, and he was working his way up from bit players to leading ladies in the repertoire company for which he and his wife served on the fund-raising committee. Because he was having sex with women whom his wife knew and with whom they socialized in addition to their activities supporting the arts, he was always on the verge of getting caught. That only added to the excitement, as John found that living on the edge was thrilling. Of course, it was also proving to be a problem. More and more of his work time was spent scheming ways to arrange extramarital meetings without his wife's knowing. Even when he had fallen in love with one of the actresses, he did not stop sleeping with as many of the others in the company as he could. His workday was now 80 percent personal affairs and 20 percent doing what he was paid for. Eventually, he was fired from the $200,000-a-year job, and his third wife divorced him shortly thereafter.

John had a very clear case of sexual addiction. Sex occupied him all day long—it was invasive, taking over his work and every other aspect of his life, and he simply could not get enough. Each new actress allowed him to feel good about himself for a day or two, and then the old gnawing would return. He would become anxious, restless, and preoccupied until he connected with someone else. I do believe that John genuinely cared about his wife and wanted to be a good husband, but he simply could not. He was obsessed with feeling good about himself because he felt so terrible. These creatures—these actresses—whom he saw as kind of magical, wanted him, and that made him feel good. He, however, did not really want them; rather, he wanted the knowledge that *they* wanted *him*. Although these relationships contained sexual pleasure, they were not about sex. They were about self-esteem and the escape from inner pain.

John hit bottom on his sexual addiction when he lost his job. The failure of his marriage was almost incidental. The idea that he, who had come from delinquent kid to successful executive, could suddenly be fired flabbergasted him. He saw no connection between losing his job and the fact that he was not doing his job. Instead, he thought that it all had to do with market forces and office politics. An important part of the therapy consisted of my connecting the consequences (the job loss) with his addiction. This took a long time, but finally he got it, and slowly he began to curb his sexual activities.

I suggested to John that he join Sexual Compulsives Anonymous (S.C.A.). He had tried A.A. off and on during his drinking years and flatly refused, saying that it was all "a bunch of bull" and that he was turned off by the religious side of the 12-step programs. I suggested that he use it as a support system even though he did not necessarily agree with all its beliefs. I tried to argue that the 12-step programs were spiritual and not religious, but it did not work—his recovery was not going to be a 12-step one; rather, he would need psychotherapy.

Eventually, although he still had affairs with actresses, the affairs lasted longer, and he was less obsessed with them. He found a job that paid much less money and involved much less responsibility, and he seemed quite satisfied. Finally, John began to open up and discuss his childhood, and I noticed a direct connection between these discussions and the subsequent improvements in his life and his feelings about himself.

I knew John for a long time before he wept in a session, but weep he did, and it freed him. He began to talk about what it was like to be in that little town where everyone knew him and his mother when his family was barely getting by. At times the whole town knew that they did not have the mortgage money, and all his friends had seen his father vomiting in the gutter. For the most part, the other boys were not cruel, but occasionally they were, and it was these incidents that were seared indelibly into John's mind and heart.

Looking back, John realized that he compensated by excelling academically. He was reassured by being smarter and more successful than the comfortable, buoyant kids who came from stable homes. Fortunately, his attempt to exact revenge—on his enabling family, his drunken father, the comfortable and sometimes mocking neighborhood kids, and the judgmental townspeople—

through theft had not hurt him nearly as much as it might have, and the compassionate judge had helped him turn his life around. John remembered that when he went to college it was easier because no one knew him or knew about his father (who died in delirium tremens during John's first year at college). The problem had been that he was still carrying within him all those years of shame. Being a successful student did not seem to mask the pain anymore, but sex and alcohol did. The sex made him feel competent, loved, lovable, and superior rather than at the bottom of the heap.

John's sexual behavior changed significantly after he got in emotional contact with the memory of being mocked while his father vomited in the street. It was not a sudden, overnight transformation; in fact, it took several years of intense therapeutic work before he started liking himself, but it was a turning point nonetheless. Today, John is married for a fourth time. He tells me that he has an occasional "chorus girl" lapse but that he is more or less faithful and content in his present marriage. This is perhaps a less than perfect recovery, but it is a recovery. John's obsession was gone, and his "slips" (relapses), however undesirable, did not trigger a return to the obsession.

Russell also succeeded in recovering from sexual addiction by using individual private therapy and a bottom-up approach. He was a distinguished man, and when he called me he mentioned his name in a way that assumed that I would recognize it. He was an extremely successful playwright and film scriptwriter who had spent many years on the police force, rising to a high rank in the Chicago Police Department. His love of Chicago and his knowledge of its history, people, neighborhoods, architecture, symbiotic relationship with Lake Michigan, and pulsing vitality was encyclopedic. I would later become acquainted with his artistic work, and when I did I could feel the love he had for his city and for what he called "the job" (the police department). I think it was his gift for articulating his love for his native city (and the police force that protected it) that enabled him to be so successful at his craft. He was able to perfectly catch the nuances of language that the cops and robbers would use in both his play and his movie scripts. Although Russell had no problem loving the city of Chicago and the Chicago law enforcement, he did have a problem loving people. Russell was involved with six women simultaneously and truly believed that he was in love with two of them. These two were pressuring him to choose between them and to settle down with one or the other.

Russell had been a sexual addict all his adult life. For the near 30 years that he worked as a police officer, he had blatantly lied to his first wife about nearly everything. Few cops have had to return so many fugitives to California or work as much overtime as Russell told his wife he had to. His wife must have been an enabler because she never challenged his blatantly improbable stories—at some level she had to have known. As a child, Russell's mother had died early, and he had been raised by a woodenly dutiful but cold stepmother. His father had a problem giving emotionally and was also physically abusive.

As an adult, Russell rationalized this as "just the way kids were treated back then," but from his descriptions of whippings with electrical cords, it sounded well beyond the culturally accepted spanking that was common during his generation. He learned early how to minimize, deny, and bury his feelings, and when he got out of high school he joined the merchant marine.

There were lots of women and some drugs, but something told him that the chemicals were too dangerous—he felt that he liked them too much. This fear worked for Russell, and once he left the merchant marine he managed never to drink or use drugs beyond occasional social use. He desperately wanted to go to medical school, but his father, who by that time was quite prosperous, refused to help him at all. He saw no possibility that he could work his way through medical school, so he took the police department entrance exam and got into law enforcement. Russell was extremely bright, and he rose rapidly. He worked with both integrity and skill, and he romanticized the police department, speaking about it as a bastion against savagery. He claimed that these officers of the law composed the only force that maintained civilization in his native city.

Although he had never thought of himself as having any sort of artistic talent and indeed looked down on such things as "sissy," he was a gifted actor and director in spite of himself. Eventually, he became involved in small theater productions. Over the years, he juggled countless women, a demanding job, a wife and kids in the suburbs, and involvement in community theater, all while attending night school to earn a degree. A big, handsome guy, he had no trouble getting partners, and he described at one point being a substitute teacher in a suburban high school to earn a few extra bucks and, as he put it, to "plank a few teachers on my desk when the kids were out of the room." Many of his exploits were strictly hit and run; yet at the same time he always had a "serious girlfriend" besides his wife. It was one such serious girlfriend who eventually led to his divorce.

After his divorce, Russell had three "serious girlfriends" plus innumerable other partners. He saw his only problem as choosing which of the three he could use for stability. He simply wanted one woman whom he could park somewhere while he continued to run around as much as he wanted.

Russell's writing career took off after he met a theater producer who had seen one of his amateur productions. When Russell and the producer spoke at a cast party, the producer invited him to write a cops-and-robbers play. Russell accepted, and the play was not only produced but also picked up by Hollywood, and he was off and running. Eventually, Russell was commuting across the country and had not only a girl in every port (as he had as a youth in the merchant marine) but dozens of girls in every port.

By now, his children were barely talking to him because they were furious at the way he had treated their mother. He was also involved in several lawsuits over his escapades with married women, had caught a venereal disease, and was getting too old to keep up his strenuous lifestyle. He finally retired from the police force because he had plenty of money from his movies. The money, however, did not bring him any happiness.

Russell's problem was about lovelessness. Russell had not been loved when it had counted, and, like Clinton, all his conquests were searches for a mother's love without risking abandonment or rejection. He sought love in a way that he could not possibly receive it. His semi-intimate relationships with wife and children were distanced by his manic quest for new partners, and of course none of these brought him any satisfaction. He rationalized everything by saying, "I've always been highly sexed," yet under his excuses lay a yawning pit of pain and anguish. Russell's sexual addiction was essentially an antidepressant—a manic defense against underlying depression.

When I first met Russell, his first statement to me was, "I'm no therapy maven. I just came here to solve a problem, and then I'll leave." You can hear the counter-dependency and the hit-and-run mentality. Get in, do the job, and get out.

Russell believed that it would be my job to help him choose which of his three candidates would win the spot for a "serious relationship." I saw my job as giving him insight into his sexual addiction. It was not an easy therapy process, but Russell slowly came to see a problem not only with selecting one woman for a serious relationship but also with the way he pursued women. I said to him, "What difference does it make who you choose, you're not going to spend any time with her anyway."

My statement got through to him, although it took another year to fully break through his denial.

I think the fact that I genuinely liked him helped the therapy enormously. He knew, although I never stated it outright, that I was fond of him, and this was unusual for him because he was used to operating in the world of show business, where true admiration is rare. He also knew that, unlike those in the world of show business, I did not seek to use or exploit him, so he did not feel threatened by me. Essentially, I had no axe to grind.

After Russell broke down the denial, the real work was putting him in touch with all his underlying pain. The sorest point was his father's refusal to help with his education. The amount of rage connected to what Russell viewed as a brutal act of denial and rejection amazed him. He had never thought of himself as an angry person; in fact, he had always felt contempt for the cops he knew who released such anger by abusing their authority.

Russell changed once he got in touch with his rage and shame at having been an unloved and unwanted child. Powerful emotions surfaced as he came to feel how his father had found him a nuisance and his stepmother barely met his basic needs and that, even when she did, she did it in a cold way. Shame, sadness, and rage were replaced in his pursuit of women with a desperate, compulsive fleeing from what was within him. Now he felt his emotions, and feeling them freed him. As he gained insight into the way he had fled pain in sexual compulsion, his acting out became rare. Eventually, Russell married one of the "candidates" and, I imagine, has been less than perfectly faithful to her, but he is certainly no longer the sexual addict he once was.

As he curtailed his sexual activities, he was amazed to find that he did not really miss his old lifestyle once he went through a period of readjustment, a period that had characteristics of chemical withdrawal. He liked himself much more as a controlled and contained sexual person. He was also surprised to discover how good sex could be with the woman he chose. He had never enjoyed sex in the way he did while in recovery.

Russell's almost manic level of energy was manifest not only in his creativity but also in his avocation of compulsive seduction. I wondered what he would do with all that energy in recovery, but it did not turn out to be a problem. He became a traveler, having the financial means to do so, and the last I heard he was enjoying himself with his wife on a Mediterranean isle.

Many addicts suffer from symptoms of posttraumatic stress disorder (PTSD), the trauma which is sometimes caused by natural disaster, accidents, assaults, wars, or earthquakes. However, in the case of addiction the trauma usually stems from physical and sexual abuse experienced as a child. In each case, the victim is emotionally numbed; tormented by intrusive thoughts, flashbacks, and the need to endlessly reenact the trauma in one way or another; and plagued by depression and anxiety. The rate of comorbidity of PTSD with addictions is extremely high.

Competing therapeutic treatments exist for PTSD, and some of these are diametrically opposed. Some strategies aim to repress the trauma and divert attention from it; others help the patient relive the experience in such a way that it will not be endlessly repeated but will be dealt with and left behind. I subscribe to the emotional-expression school because I do not think that the diversion-suppression techniques really accomplish anything. Although one would think that the last thing trauma victims need is to mentally revisit scenes of past trauma endlessly, I have found that the presence of a therapist transforms the experience from compulsive repetition to meaningful integration. The compulsive acting out of a trauma is very different from experiencing pain in the presence of an empathic other.

The treatment of PTSD involves pulling the traumatic experience into the mainframe of self so that it feels not alien but rather a part of one's life. It is also important to help the patient give meaning to the experience, to understand it. This technique has proven to help those who have been abused as children. Bill Clinton still harbors unacknowledged traumatization, however much he denies it. Arguing that having an alcoholic stepfather is far from the worst of traumas does not mean that the trauma did not occur.

Trauma isolates us from the rest of our experience. The part of us that has been traumatized is experienced almost as another person, and the same idea applies to those with addictions. The sexual addict is a different person from the rest of the person. As the following case illustrates, Sister Ellen was both a caring, magnificently skilled teacher who communicated her love of literature to her students and a guilt-ridden, emotionally alone, compulsive masturbater.

Sister Ellen, a member of a Catholic teaching order, had been sexually abused as a child, and both her parents were alcoholic. When her working-class Irish parents would come home from a drinking bout, they would be cursing, fighting, and in danger of injuring each other. From an early age, Sister Ellen and her younger brother would form a wedge between the drunken parents, separating them as they led them to bed. The younger brother would remain with the mother, and Sister Ellen would sleep with her father. When she was barely pubescent, her father began to fondle her, and she responded with sexual arousal. Although no intercourse took place, this repeated experience spoiled sex for her for the rest of her life. Because such intense and conflicted feelings arose, she did the opposite of what a sexual addict does—she renounced sex with other people.

Sister Ellen came to me with panic disorder, suffering debilitating anxiety attacks that made it difficult for her to stay in the classroom or attend meetings. She had long since given up traveling or going far from the school where she taught. She had never told anyone her guilty secret about what went on with her father. Additionally, although she had renounced sex, she became a compulsive masturbater, like Ted. Her fantasies were overwhelmingly homosexual, and she felt incredibly guilty about them.

People are homosexual for a variety of reasons—genetic predisposition being the most powerful and perhaps most common reason—although our knowledge in this area is scant. I do not think that Sister Ellen was a born homosexual. I think her homosexuality was defensive because to have sexual fantasies about men was to have sexual fantasies about father, and this was simply too upsetting. Therefore, she changed her focus to women but was ashamed of that as well. It also tormented her with guilt. As are so many sexual compulsives, she was cross-addicted, in this case to alcohol and food.

Sister Ellen had gone to a school run by the teaching order that she now belonged to and with which she had found love and support almost immediately. She was an academically gifted student from an early age, and the nuns in elementary school and the sisters in high school had provided her with a lot of the emotional nurturing she simply could not get from her addicted parents. It was a natural step to go on to joining the order. All that was healthy. What was not healthy was the burying of the conscious (but unacknowledged) trauma and the addictions that she used to stave off the unconscious feelings about the trauma.

Sister Ellen was an extraordinarily likable person. I sometimes envied her students because her love of the literature that she taught and her ability to convey that love were so clear. It even came through in the therapy sessions. She was a born teacher, and joining a teaching order, although it was a choice made in fear and in flight, had been an excellent vocational choice.

Sister Ellen liked to quote the founder of her order to the effect that "Work is prayer." And she was my kind of gal, committed to something she cared about and doing it well. For all my admiration of her, she had a terrible time feeling good about herself. Because of her masturbation, she felt that she was a hypocrite—violating her vow of chastity while presenting herself as a devout nun—and out of control. Her panic disorder resolved fairly quickly once she came for treatment. She formed a strong attachment to me, which gave her a sense of security that had been lacking all her life. The strength of that bond enabled her to trust, and in trusting she was able to talk about what had happened over a period of many years with her father. The more she talked about her traumatization, the less panic stricken she was. But the attacks did not stop until she got in contact with her rage. In one session she started screaming, "How could my father do that to a kid, no matter how drunk he was? I know my mother was no bargain, but why did my father have to take it out on me? He was cruel. *Screw him! I hate him!*" Much later in therapy, Sister Ellen was able to forgive her father and feel compassion toward him and his addiction, but the road to forgiveness had not been easy. She had to go through her rage and hatred; otherwise, the forgiveness of her father would have been phony and another form of denial.

I do not agree that forgiveness of abuse is a necessary part of healing. To be obsessed with hatred is crippling in its own way. Nevertheless, better to hate your tormentors than to unconsciously reenact the torment by turning the passive into the active. Doing so only gets the addict into a position of victimization over and over again.

For Sister Ellen, a great deal of her panic was driven by an unconscious fear of losing control of her rage. She was afraid that she would murder someone, and I believe that she had enough anger to do so. She did a lot of screaming and hollering and pounding of pillows in my office, and this release worked. The panic attacks abated, and although she lived in fear of their return, they did not come back. Her other addictions were not so easily treated. Although she did not completely overcome any of them, she greatly improved. Her drinking became more episodic and less disabling, and she gained some control over her eating (getting her weight down to where it was not an immediate health hazard). Although her sexual fantasies remained mainly homosexual, her understanding of their defensive nature made her a lot more comfortable. She now understood that her fear of having sexual thoughts about men was a result of her fear of remembering that she had been turned on by her father.

Another source of her panic was her fear that her guilt-ridden sexual fantasy life would be discovered. Masturbation became less exclusively a vehicle for reassurance and feeling better about herself. In fact, as she felt better and better about herself, she masturbated less and less, and when she masturbated, she enjoyed it more and more. She was now responding to a biological need and not hooking all kinds of extraneous freight onto that biological need. Although many of her colleagues had left the order and married, she decided that she was too far along in life to make such a radical change, and her decision to practice a kind of modified chastity made her content with her decision.

Sister Ellen's rage abated as she came to see that her parents had been overwhelmed by their attempt to get a foothold in a new country and by their alcoholism and that they had, in their own way, done the best that they could for their children, despite their grievous failures. Ellen was able to see her experience as making some kind of sense—as having some kind of meaning and relationship to her culture, to what was happening in the world during her life, and to the kinds of traumas that her parents experienced—and she ceased to feel victimized. She came to accept a certain inevitability about her traumatic experiences and to assume some responsibility for what she did with the emotional consequences of that experience. All this gave her a much greater sense of control and much less of a need to use alcohol, food, and sex compulsively.

What else is available for those who need help recovering from a sexual addiction? In addition to private individual therapy, private therapy groups exist. These are run by mental health professionals who specialize in addiction. They might be psychiatrists, psychologists, social workers, or counselors, and the groups are issue focused. Today, most insurance companies and managed care groups maintain lists of therapists who can be contacted to see whether they specialize in sexual addiction. In turn, these specialists might be able to refer individuals to private therapy groups if they do not run one themselves. In addition to the insurance lists, you can find names of therapists by consulting the local Yellow Pages under "Counselors," "Psychologists," or "Social Workers." Again, if the professional you call does not run a private therapy group, he or she can still refer you to one.

Some people use a combination of recovery programs. For example, one might join a 12-step fellowship and see a private therapist. People in recovery often come up with their own strategies to help them deal with their lives of impulse and erotic urges. It is true that some self-made strategies work, but some do not. Some addicts try to substitute sexual pleasure with another pleasure. However, this must be done with caution, or addicts might acquire a second addiction.

Addicts have been known to become extremely creative in inventing their own recovery strategies. They are not always successful, but they are creative nevertheless. Richard, a 40-something-year-old married man with a family, had a long history of hitting on younger women (including those in his workplace). His sexual advances toward women who did not welcome them led to his seeking treatment. For the first time, he was in danger of losing his job as a result of his sexual behavior because the women at work had started to complain to superiors about his advances. Previous negative consequences of

Richard's behavior included multiple threats of divorce from his wife.

During one session, Richard spontaneously offered the following recovery plan:

> Doctor, what I'm going to do is this. I'm only going to allow myself to come on to women I don't find attractive. I resolve not to have sex with anyone who turns me on, so I guess I'll only be seducing ugly women. That's even kind of an act of kindness, isn't it, Doctor? I think I could feel good about myself if I only did that, and maybe after a while I won't have to do that, either. But for now, I'll only have sex with unattractive women, and I'll only use positions I don't really enjoy. I'll also do things I don't really enjoy, such as performing cunnilingus. What do you think, do you think my plan will help me recover?

At first, I thought he was putting me on, but he was not. I threw his question back at him, asking him whether *he* thought it would work. As we struggled to elaborate his plan, I realized that Richard's thought processes were far from realistic.

Obviously, this recovery plan did not work, and Richard dropped out of treatment shortly after his wife filed for divorce. He might have been in treatment only to placate her. Although people ultimately must recover for themselves, it is true that most addicts initially come for treatment because they "have to," often under the threat of job loss or divorce. At first they are in recovery for someone else; only later will they be there for themselves. Although Richard's attempt at creative self-help did not work, Mike's did. Mike was referred to me by his nurse-practitioner girlfriend who was distraught over his return to drinking. He was a Vietnam War veteran who had been sober for eight years but returned to drinking several months before he appeared in my office—inarticulate, obviously very shook up, and strangely menacing and timid at the same time. He was a big fellow, and he was sitting on a lot of internalized rage. In fact, I was slightly afraid of both him and his rage. He was especially angry at his last therapist, who he felt had not helped him at all, a relationship that I did not comment on. He proceeded to tell me the following story:

I live in a very rural area. There's not much around my house. A few months back I was sitting on my back deck feeling really nervous. The Gulf War had just broken out, and I was listening to the news reports. All I could think about was body bags—all the guys who were going to be sent out in body bags. Then I thought I heard something in the trees at the back of my property. And then they started coming. It felt like the Vietcong were coming out of the bushes. I knew it wasn't real, but I couldn't really stop it, so I hid under my deck. When I came out, I got a six-pack of beer, and I've been drinking ever since. I hate drinking.

When I was in Vietnam we drank a lot and used other drugs, you know how it is, and we went to the whorehouses as often as we could. There was a lot of sex and a lot of drugs, and I came back and got married. It didn't work out. Well, I drank a lot, and I guess I cheated a lot too, but, you know, it wasn't much of a marriage. I didn't know what I was doing when I got out of the service. I've got a couple of boys; they're angry at me, I guess, and they don't really talk to me. They're in college now. I tried to be a good husband and father, but you know how it is, you're hanging out in the bar, there's some floozy there, she'll go down on you, she'll go to a room with you, or whatever. I did a lot of that stuff. But then the booze got me.

There's a lot of alcoholism in my family. One of my brothers died of cirrhosis, and our dad, he was really messed up. Some of my uncles too, and yeah, I guess my grandfather. Anyway, I got it—alcoholism. I knew I had to stop drinking or I was going to get in bad trouble. You know I did some heroin in Nam, too—everyone did— but I never did that when I came back. Some pot some-times, but what I really liked was the booze and the gals. I stopped drinking when I was starting to miss work and I felt really sick.

I'm an engineer, and I'm involved in weapons pro-duction, so I have a lot of contact with the military. I don't like it because I don't like some of the things that happened in Nam. Nobody likes to hear war stories, so I won't tell you any, but I saw a lot of stuff, and I guess I did a lot of stuff, too. But I don't talk about that.

Anyway, I did stop drinking. I went to A.A. I was never, you know, a real groupie or nothing, but I went to meetings for a few years, and then I stopped going to meetings. Well, I continued to go occasionally—to a friend's anniversary or something like that—but I was not in it big time. But I didn't drink. Once I wasn't drinking, I had problems being with other women, so that stopped, too. And then came the divorce. I was really hurt by that—I thought she'd be happy with me once I stopped drinking, and I didn't go back to it after my marriage broke up. I moved East and got this job with this defense company. The trouble with the boys is they think I didn't give them enough money for school. I think I did; I've been generous with them.

I do have trouble with my feelings, and I'm not a very emotional guy. It's not that I didn't love my sons, but I couldn't show it. I guess their mom has her reasons for getting rid of me, but I really was a much better husband after I stopped drinking.

Anyway, I came East, and I started this affair with this nurse, and I guess she's more into me than I'm into her. Well, we've had a few fights about action on the side, but that hasn't been too big. The thing was, when I heard that newscast I just couldn't get the body bags out of my mind. Gee, I know there wasn't anyone really coming out of the woods in my backyard; I was just upset, but it felt like they were.

Now—this is what I can't stand—I'm fine at work. Once I'm there, I don't want to drink, and I never drink at lunch, even though some of the guys do. It's not a problem for me, but once I get in my car and I'm coming home, I tell myself, "I'm going to go home and I'm not going to drink tonight because it makes me feel really sick." But the next morning, I'm hung over and depressed, and I hate myself when I do it. I always say I'm not going to do it, but when I get to the town just before my house, it's like the car drives itself to the bar. Once I'm there, I say, "Well, I'm just going to have a beer," but two hours later I'm still in there drinking and buying a six-pack to take home. Sometimes I pick someone up, and I don't want to do that, either.

You know, I don't care about Sarah as much as she cares about me, but I don't want to hurt her or anything. I'd just break off with her if I was going to do that. Though more often than not, I don't go home at all. When I do go home, it's either with beer or another person. Sometimes I'll find someone at the bar, and we'll do something in the back room. You know how it is, I go in cheap places; I guess there are cheap women there. Even though I don't want to do those things, I do them anyway. I don't want to drink, and I don't even care about the sex, but I do both, and I don't even know why. I mean it feels good, but I don't understand it. When I'm driving back from my work, and I'm coming down the highway, I think I see things in my peripheral vision on both sides of the highway. I don't know if they are Vietcong or not. And then the goddamn car drives itself to this bar. You don't know how I hate myself in the morning. It's not me. I don't know how it happens.

When I suggested that Mike drank and sometimes spent the night with women because he was afraid to go home and see the Vietcong come out of the trees again, he vehemently denied it, insisting that there was no connection whatsoever—he was just "weak." As therapy progressed, Mike became increasingly depressed and filled with self-hatred for being weak and for having the car drive him to the bar or, sometimes, to the beer distributor to buy a case. He truly experienced the whole process as involuntary—in fact, against his will. A more vivid example of being out of control would be difficult to find.

Being out of control bothered Mike more than anything else and seemed to be fueling his depression. We made no progress over the next couple of months. The only thing that changed was the depth of Mike's depression. I started to worry about his committing suicide. At that point, I told him about a drug called Antabuse. This drug has no effect if you do not drink, but it makes you deathly ill if you do. I urged him to see a psychiatrist and get a prescription. I had made other suggestions, such as trying antidepressant medication, going to a posttraumatic stress group at the VA hospital, and returning to A.A. I was not able to sell any of my ideas, and Mike's life remained much the same as his depression worsened. I was surprised that he was quite enthusiastic about going on Antabuse. Although I was somewhat hesitant to recommend the drug (without the alcohol and the sexual escapades he might "lose it" and become overtly psychotic), I figured that little was to be lost, as his present condition was deteriorating rapidly. If he had a psychotic break while he was sober and home alone, he would be admitted to a hospital and perhaps get the treatment he needed to start life over again on a steadier, firmer basis.

Fortunately, such a psychotic episode never took place. Mike was delighted that he could not drink while on the Antabuse. He was nervous at home, but he never again saw the Vietcong coming out of the trees. His depression significantly lifted, because he no longer felt out of control, though he was furious at his previous therapist for not having suggested Antabuse. His sexual acting out also ceased. Not going to the bar, he had little opportunity for sex. Although he complained of boredom, he did not return to the bars to pick up women because he was afraid of drinking while taking the Antabuse. It was as if the Antabuse worked for his sexual and his drinking compulsion, or at least he connected the two in his mind.

The therapy changed now, and he began talking about his experiences in Vietnam. He had seen beloved fellow officers mutilated and killed. Although I never heard the full extent of what happened, it became clear that he had been involved in various atrocities. Under the conditions, the degree of his culpability was in question, but he himself was harshly condemning of his role in the war. Although his alcoholism and perhaps his sexual addiction clearly had some genetic determinants, this PTSD and his attempt to self-medicate it were also powerful determinants of his addiction. All the alcoholism in his family meant that he came into the world with a nervous system predisposed to addictions, not only to that of alcohol but to addiction in general. However, neurochemistry is not necessarily destiny. It merely provides vulnerability to the addiction. As it turned out, Mike experienced more than a little trauma in his childhood and then suffered the gross, prolonged traumatization of war during his years in Vietnam. He had literally never spoken to anyone about the things that had happened to him and that he had been involved in. Rather, he drank and sexed those feelings away. So strenuously had Mike tried to repress those painful memories and emotions that he was unable to allow himself to feel much of anything. Being a very bright and talented man, he was able to perform at a high level at work but poorly as husband, father, and boyfriend. It was a tragic scenario.

Although Mike had a great deal of work to do, it looked as though he was on the road to recovery when his firm closed its local operation and transferred him to a distant state. I urged him to return to therapy there, but, having never heard from him, I do not know whether that happened. An interesting wrinkle occurred in Mike's recovery. It seemed extremely important for him to attribute the change he was undergoing solely to the Antabuse. It was as though he was afraid to take any responsibility for his recovery, despite the fact that he was choosing to take the medicine and was very active in his recovery. I think this happened because of his guilt and because he did not trust himself. He felt that he did not deserve to recover because of the things he had seen and done in combat, but if something else was responsible for his recovery, that would be okay. He could get the benefit of the medicine as long as he did not have to take any credit for his recovery because, at a gut level, he was certain that he did not deserve to be well. *Guilt and shame keep people pursuing their obsessions with substances and compulsive activities.*

Mike's unconsciously creative way of not working through his guilt and shame but subverting it and going around it worked for him. It was not an ideal solution, but it was a solution. It was also important to him that he not give me any credit for helping his recovery: to do so would threaten him by bringing up feelings of closeness and gratitude to me. That was simply too dangerous from his perspective because I might die, just as his buddies in Vietnam had. He was not going to get close to anyone, male or female, wife, girlfriend, or child. That was really sad, and it is my hope that Mike, who has already overcome a great deal in choosing to take the Antabuse and to cease the drinking and sexing, will be able to move on and once again become a feeling human being.

At first glance, it would appear that both Mike and Bill Clinton have absolutely nothing in common. However, like Mike, Clinton was born with a genetic vulnerability to addiction and experienced both childhood trauma and severe stress—all of which predisposed him to addiction.

Why do some addicts recover while others do not? This is not an easy question to answer. Addicts in 12-step programs speak of having wondered, "Why me?" when they were suffering from their addictions and the negative consequences of those addictions. When this question is posed at this time in the addict's life, it is framed from a point of view of being victimized: "Why did I end up this way?" Later, once they are in recovery, they again ask, "Why me?" only now it is no longer from a victim's perspective. Now, "Why me?" means "Why did I choose life while others literally pursue their addictions to death?" No one really knows why certain people recover and others do not. Even after 20 years of working with addicts, I am constantly surprised by those who make it and those who do not.

This is not to say that some people are capable of recovery and others are not. In fact, I believe that every addict is capable of recovery. The problem is that the ability to do so requires the addict to look into the abyss and to experience some pretty god-awful pain. Therefore, what can therapists do to enable that recovery? They can provide support, education, insight, coping skills, and strategies. Sometimes therapists need the heavy artillery—individual, group, self-, family, and pharmaceutical help all combined—but are too reluctant to use it. In these days of managed care, there is less and less money to pay for the heavy artillery, but addictions are a matter of life and death. Going into debt in order to rehabilitate—to save your life—is as good as investments get.

My own experience with recovering addicts is that two tasks seem to help them the most: mourning losses and getting aggression out front. It is true that one cannot mourn behind an addiction because the addiction anesthetizes in a way that makes it very difficult to feel grief with sufficient depth in order to work it through and leave it behind. The work of mourning involves making those we have lost part of us so that we can say goodbye to them. I have already suggested that Bill Clinton was unable to mourn the many loses in his life in a way that he was able to come to terms with them.

In treating addict after addict, I have found that almost all of them have losses that they have not adequately mourned, including life opportunities lost as a result of their addictions. We mourn for ourselves as well as for others—or at least we can. That mourning work, painful as it is, is liberating.

The second task that I have found to be extremely helpful deals with aggression. Addicts must get their aggression out front instead of keeping it inside. If they do not, the aggression turns inward—against the self—and deprives addicts of the energy they need to pursue their goals. Such inward aggression serves only to fuel self-destructive behaviors such as sexual addiction. Clinton appears to externalize his aggression by using it to achieve his goals. Although this appears to be a healthy externalization, I believe that it is deceptive. As we saw in Chapter Four, all of Clinton's biographers have noted that he was a rageful man while governor. As president, he appears to have learned to keep his rage under wraps, but I cannot help but wonder how much of his rage, especially against women, finds expression in his addiction. I also wonder how much he is motivated down a path of self-destruction by the need to punish himself for forbidden aggression—aggression against all the women who, at some level, must represent his mother.

Depending on which stage of recovery an addict is in, the addiction can be viewed as either *ego-alien* or *ego-syntonic,* the difference being in the addict's perception. Addicts who recognize their addictions and view them as separate from their true self—as discordant with their self-concept—have an ego-alien addiction. However, addicts who see their behavior not as an addiction but simply as a part of who they are have an ego-syntonic condition. Recognizing that a problem exists is always the first step in recovery, so those who see the problem (ego-alien) are further ahead in the game than those who do not see the problem (ego-syntonic).

Grandiosity (the belief that "the rules don't apply to me, I'm special, I'm entitled") reinforces denial and keeps addictions ego-alien. If the addict is a president, then reality confirms the grandiose self-perception. Henry Adams, historian and descendent of Presidents John Adams and John Quincy Adams, tells us in his autobiography: *The Education of Henry Adams,*

Power is poison. Its effects on Presidents has always been tragic, chiefly as an almost insane excitement at first, and as worse reaction afterwards; but also because no mind is so well balanced as to bear the strain of seizing unlimited force without habit or knowledge of it; and finding it disputed with him by hungry packs of wolves and hounds whose lives depend on snatching the carrion.

Grandiosity must be relinquished before recovery can occur. That would be difficult but not impossible for a president, and Clinton, like any other addict, is capable of recovering.

What does recovery feel like? In recovery, a person is more him- or herself, meaning that identity is restored and that he or she has more of a sense of individuality, uniqueness, or separation from others. The addict realizes that, in some ultimate way, we are born alone and die alone, and yet, paradoxically and at the same time, he or she feels more at one with others, more a "part of the main." There is more of a realization and an experience of what the poet Dylan Thomas, himself to die of his alcohol addiction, was talking about when he said, "The force which through the green fields drives the flower, drives me." The addict feels more relaxed, less anxious, more free, and more peaceful. One of the best things about recovery is that trust issues become easier because no one has anything on you, so you need not be afraid of anyone exploiting or betraying you. The freedom inherent in that is simply marvelous, and no less marvelous are the good feelings about yourself that result.

However, recovery is not utopia. It is a better place, but it is not an ideal place. Recovering people, regardless of their addictions, must still face all the dilemmas of human life. Just like the rest of us, they must face disappointment, internal conflicts, sickness, aging, and death. But they do so from a much better perspective than they ever could have when they still were in the throes of addiction. This would be true for a recovering Bill Clinton as well. Nothing would go away—all the issues of his life, all his childhood baggage, and all his present responsibilities would be there, but he would be in a far better position to deal with each of them. He, too, could have some of those wonderful feelings of freedom and peace with himself that so many recovering people report.

Now, one could argue that a more restrained sexual life would not necessarily mean absolute fidelity, depending on the understanding between spouses, but for Clinton it would at least mean an end to sexual kleptomania. It is possible to have democratic leaders whose sexual behavior might not be classified as heterosexual monogamy but still is not driven, compulsive, and out of control.

A Clinton in recovery would be a Clinton without an "integrity problem." His recovery would certainly entail being more faithful to his wife, and it would not have the "spinning-out-of-control craziness" that the press and other media have recently treated us to. He would be a president with the time to devote to the destiny of the nation—the time the nation deserves. He would be a president who could more easily take principled stands, and he would be far freer from the compulsion to tell people what they wanted to hear. He would be not only a better leader but a happier man as well, and that would be a great change in a political leader—a change both at the human level and in the way he conducts his job and leads our country.

Would Mr. Clinton need to go into therapy? It would certainly be a good idea. I cannot quite see the Secret Service going into local S.C.A. meetings in Washington, but then again, why not? We could have the 1600 Pennsylvania Avenue Group, and members could come to the White House for meetings.

Certainly, being in individual therapy would not be a political problem in any way for the president. Both Bill Clinton and Vice President Al Gore have spoken favorably of psychotherapy. In fact, Gore has talked about how much it helped him following his son's illness. Counseling or psychotherapy could definitely help, as could joining ACOA (Adult Children of Alcoholics) to deal with the issues that Clinton clearly has not worked through. You do not grow up surrounded by addiction in the way Clinton did and walk away scot-free. Both his political style and his personal life have been affected in detrimental ways. As such, the president would do the nation a great service by admitting that he needs help, by getting that help, and by being open about his addiction. What a wonderful model that would be. It would free up millions of Americans to get the help they need for their addictions, including sexual addiction.

AFTERWORD

WHAT, YOU MAY ASK, are my convictions and conclusions about all this? Well, they are rather simple. Now, as was true when I began writing this book, I am not sure what Bill Clinton did or did not do, and neither is anyone else, with the exception of Bill Clinton. However, on the basis of the evidence (controversial as it is), I would conclude that Clinton does have a problem with sex and that that problem has led him to do impulsive, dangerous things that make little sense. His actions suggest a drivenness and compulsiveness that certainly have the overtones of an addiction.

The inner child, as discussed in detail by television personality and addictions specialist John Bradshaw, really does exist. It is getting in touch with that inner child and its pain that frees us as adults to move on from the compulsions and addictions we all have. Doing this allows us to be in the here and now rather than reenacting the there and then of childhood injury, shame, and pain. This is no less true for President Clinton than it is for the rest of us.

My own view is that we all have conflicts, pain, and unresolved issues, many of which date back to early trauma. We could all use help in handling these feelings, especially those of us who are in positions of great responsibility, because such responsibility brings all kinds of additional stress into our lives.

It is interesting to note that the defining slogan of Bill Clinton's generation was "Make love, not war." Clinton seems to have both embodied and incarnated that slogan. As a nation, I believe that we are grateful that he has not made war even as we question if he has made too much love. I also believe that as a nation we have, in a sense, become voyeuristic sexual addicts, hanging on every word from the latest bimbo and every revelation in a prurient way that is almost as unhealthy as having a primary addiction. Aside from the kick that the country seems to be getting out of the whole matter, and despite Clinton's high ratings as president, the problem with our national obsession is not only that it becomes a vicarious sexual addiction of its own but also that it easily leads to a self-righteous judgmental attitude that we could well do without as individuals and as a nation. One might argue that because I have written a book whose sales will depend on appealing to that vicarious interest in our leader's sexual life, I could be accused of hypocrisy on this issue. To those I reply, I am only human, just like you, and despite my own conflicting views on this matter, it is my sincere hope that I have not been leering or encouraged others to leer. Rather, I hope that I have offered an explanation that makes sense of what seems to be truly crazy behavior and enlightens the entire problem of sexual addiction.

Afterword

Mr. President, if indeed you are the innocent victim of political vindictiveness, you have my deepest, most profound apologies. On the other hand, if you have the problem that I think you have, and any or all the shoes displayed in this book fit, I urge you to get help for yourself. You need not do this publicly nor make any public confession if you think that unwise or politically suicidal. However, my belief is that going public would raise your ratings. In any case, I wish you well and continue to be your (not uncritical) admirer.

And readers, if you or a loved one suffers from sexual addiction, I urge you to get help for yourself or your loved one. Addictions are treatable disorders.

BIBLIOGRAPHY

Alcoholics Anonymous World Services. 1952. *Twelve Steps and Twelve Traditions.* New York: Alcoholics Anonymous.

Allen, Charles and Jonathan Portis. 1992. *The Comeback Kid: The Life and Career of Bill Clinton.* New York: Birch Lane Press.

American Psychiatric Association. 1994. *Diagnostic and Statistical Manual of Mental Disorders,* Forth Edition. Washington D.C. :APA.

Bradshaw, John. 1988. *Healing the Shame That Binds You.* Dearfield Beach, Fl: Health Communications.

Carnes, Patrick. 1991. *Don't Call It Love.* New York: Bantam Books.

Carnes, Patrick. 1992. *Out of the Shadows.* Center City, Minnesota: Hazelden Foundation.

Erikson, Erik. 1963. *Childhood and Society.* New York: Norton.

Erikson, Erik. 1969. *Ghandi's Truth.* New York: Norton.

Fick, Paul. 1995. *The Dysfunctional President: Inside the Mind of Bill Clinton.* New York: Birch Lane Press.

Fromm, Erich. 1941. *Escape from Freedom.* New York: Reinhart.

Bibliography

Goodman, Ariel "Diagnosis and Treatment of Sexual Addiction." *Sex and Marital Therapy*. 19 (1993): 225–251.

Khantzian, Edward J. 1981. *Some Treatment Implications of Ego and Self-Disturbances in Alcoholism in Dynamic Approaches to the Understanding and Treatment of Alcoholism*. New York: Free Press.

Kohut, Heinz 1971. *The Analysis of Self.* New York: International University Press.

Kohut, Heinz 1977. *Preface to Psychodynamics of Drug Dependence*. Washington DC: U.S. Government Printing Service.

Levin. Jerome D. 1991. *Recovering from Alcoholism: Beyond Your Wildest Dreams*. Northvale, NY: Jason Aronson.

Levin, Jerome D. 1987. *Treatment of Alcoholism and other Addictions: A Self-Psychology Approach*. Northvale, NJ: Jason Aronson.

Maraniss, David. 1996. *First in His Class*. New York: Simon & Schuster.

Miller, Alice. 1981. *The Drama of the Gifted Child*. Also published as *Prisoners of Childhood,* trans. R. Ward. New York: Basic Books.

Tyrell, Jr., R. Emmett. 1996. *Boy Clinton: The Political Biography*. Washington DC: Regnery Publishing Inc.

Winnicott, Donald. 1958. *"The Capacity to Be Alone." The Maturational Processes and the Facilitating Environment*. New York: International University Press.

INDEX

A

Abandonment depression, 70
Abstinence, 157–158
  from alcohol, 165
Acting out, 199–200
Adams, Henry, 236
Adams, John Quincy, 236
Addictions
  as biphasic, 130–131
  bottom-up approach to,
    153–154
  consequences and, 209
  cycle of, 85
  defined, 26
  denial as pathognomic of,
    106
  ego-alien addiction, 236
  ego-syntonic addiction, 236
  identification with the ag-
    gressor, 82–83
  negative consequences of,
    130–131
  polyaddiction, 160
  as self-medication, 131–132
  shame and, 197–198
  top-down approach to,
    153–154
Adult child of alcoholics
  (ACOA), 19, 66, 91–92
  political expression and, 125

Adult Children of Alcoholics
  (ACOA), 196, 239
Aggression. See Rage
AIDS, 199–200
Alcoholics Anonymous (A.A.),
    61, 177–183
  closed meetings, 180–181
  curative elements of,
    179–180
  open meetings, 180
Alcoholism, 26
  of Clinton, Roger, 64
  depression and, 197
  families, alcoholic, 13–14
  veterans and, 226–233
Alexithymia, 56–57
Allegations of sexual encoun-
    ters, 100–101
Allen, Charles, xiv
Allen, Woody, 125
Amazon.com, 24
American Psychiatric Associa-
    tion (APA), 25
The American Spectator, 98
Anal intercourse, 199, 200
Anger. See Rage
Angry scale, 88
Antabuse, 230–231
Antidepressant, sex as, 32–33
Antiwar movement, 78

Index

Anxiety disorders, 154
Approval, search for, 116–117
Archaic nuclear self, 112
Arkansas Industrial Development Commission, 94
Arkansas State Troopers, 87, 88, 98, 144
Attention-deficit disorder (ADD), 154
Attorney general of Arkansas, 85–86

B

Baird, Zoe, 120
Behavioral treatment of addiction, 155
Bennett, Robert, 101, 105–106
Bestiality, 167, 172
Biological determinants, 42
    Clinton, Bill and, 64
Biphasic, addictions as, 130–131
Blackouts, 206
Blythe, William Jefferson, 15, 45–46
    death of, 46
    as sensation seeker, 54
Bonding, 47–48
Boss Tweed, 126
Bottom-up approaches, 153–154
Bowen, Murray, 44
Boy Clinton: The Political Biography (Tyrrell), xiv–xv
Bradshaw, John, 241
Brain chemistry, 42
Brock, David, 98, 144

Brown, Ron, 15, 98, 104, 123
    loss of, 17

C

Capone, Al, 53
Carnes, Patrick, 24
Cassidy, Edith, 44–45
    Clinton, Bill and, 47–49
Cassidy, Eldridge, 44
    Clinton, Bill and, 47–48, 50
Cassidy, Virginia. *See* Kelly, Virginia
Cave, myth of the, 160
Charm, 116
Childhood of Clinton, 46–47
Church activities, 90
Cigarette smoking, 141–142
Citizen Kane, 60–61
Civil actions, 29–30
Clement VII, 9
Cleopatra, 9
Clinton, Chelsea Victoria, 87
Clinton, Hillary Rodham, 10
    "deal" with Clinton, 172
    divorce, possibility of, 146
    Kelly, Virginia and, 81–82
    marriage to Clinton, 84–85
    meeting Clinton, 79–80
    support for Clinton, 143–144
Clinton, Raymond, 53, 90–91
Clinton, Roger, 15, 51–52, 90–91
    abusiveness of, 62
    alcoholism of, 64
    death of, 75–76
    divorce of, 63

remarriage to Kelly, Virginia, 63

violence of, 51, 52–53

Clinton, Roger Cassidy, 59

drug problem of, 90–91

Clinton, Virginia. *See* Kelly, Virginia

Co-addicts, 48

Co-dependents, 48

The Comeback Kid: The Life and Career of Bill Clinton (Allen & Portis), xiv

Communication

gift for, 152

sex and, 156

Comorbidities, 154

posttraumatic stress disorder (PTSD) and, 217–219

Compassion, 221

Compulsive, addictions as, 93–94

Conditional love, 110

Confession, 187

Confusion, 112

Congressional campaign, 82–84

Consequences and addiction, 209

Consistency, 124

Conversion experience, 178

Cooper, Alvin, 5

Corbin, Paula. *See* Jones, Paula Corbin

Counterdependency, 104, 215

Criteria for addiction

Diagnostic and Statistical Manual (DSM), 27–40

formal diagnosis, criteria for, 38–39

World Health Organization (WHO), 38

Cross-addiction, 160

recovery from, 161–164

12–step program and, 188–189

Crowd, working the, 115–116

Cults, 159

D

Dangerous situations, 28–29

Deceptiveness, 123

Defense mechanisms, 55

identification with the aggressor, 82–83

terminal uniqueness, 62

turning passive into active, 164

Defensive styles, 57

Denial, 213

of addiction, 43–44

breaking down of, 184, 194

Clinton, Bill and, 57

grandiosity and, 236–237

Jones, Paula Corbin and, 106

of Kelly, Virginia, 63

as pathognomic of addiction, 106

12–step program and, 181–185

Willey, Kathleen and, 101

Dependency, 26, 103

Dependency conflict theory, 103–104, 137

Index

Depression, 154
  antidepressant medications,
    230–231
  out-of-control and, 230–231
Dershowitz, Alan, 107
Devaluing comments, 198
Dewey, Thomas, 121
Diagnosis of problem, 175
Diagnostic and Statistical Manual (DSM), 25–26
  criteria for diagnosis, 27–40
Disappointments, 204
Dishonesty, 55–56
Dizziness of freedom, 159
Dole, Bob, 18
Don Giovanni, 105
Don't ask, don't tell policy, 120
Don't Call It Love: Recovery from Sexual Addiction (Carnes), 22
Dowd, Maureen, 125
Draft evasion, 16
Drug addiction, 26
  of Clinton, Roger Cassidy, 90–91
  recovery from, 157
  self-destruction and, 132–133
Dynamic treatment of addiction, 155
Dysfunctional families, 13–14
  reality, distortion of, 55
  roles in, 59–60
  use of phrase, 41–42
The Dysfunctional President (Flick), xiv
Dysthmia, 154

E

The Education of Henry Adams (Adams), 236
Ego, 4
Ego-alien addiction, 236
Ego deficits, 114
Ego-syntonic addiction, 236
Eisenhower, Dwight D., 137
  infidelity of, 139
Eisenhower, Mamie, 139
Ellis, Albert, 72
Emerson, Ralph Waldo, 124
Emotional arrest, 92
Emotional capacity, 99
Emotional impoverishment, 35
Emotional incest, 50
Empathy, 124–125
Enabler, 48–49
  Clinton, Hillary Rodham as, 80, 84
  Kelly, Virginia as, 52
Entitlement
  as coping mechanism, 88–89
  feelings of, 88
Environmental issues, 118
Erikson, Erik, 3
  eight stages of human growth, 47
Eros, 127
Escalation of need, 29
Escape from Freedom (Fromm), 158–159
Ethics and morality, 3–4
Exodus, 159
Exploitation, 123
  in relationships, 114

Index

Externalizers, 57
Extramarital affairs. *See* Infidelity

F

Failure, 72
Falwell, Jerry, 5, 144
Families. *See also* Dysfunctional families
   as imperfect, 41–42
   as social influence, 43
Fantasies, homosexual, 219–220
Father figures, 15–16
   disappointments with, 73
Fellatio. *See* Oral sex
Fick, Paul, xiv
First in His Class (Maraniss), xiv, 19
Flowers, Gennifer, 11, 86, 143
   media coverage of, 94
Forgiveness, 221–222
Foster, Vincent, 144
Fragmented self, 112
Fragmenting, 190
Freud, Sigmund, 57, 60–61
   repetition compulsion, 164
   working through theory, 91–92
Fromm, Erich, 158–159
Fulbright, Senator William, 74–75, 76

G

Gamblers Anonymous (G.A.), 182
Gambling, 53–54, 182

Gandhi's Truth (Erikson), 3
Genetics, 42
Genogram, 44
Geographic cure, 134
Georgetown University, 74
   president of student council, election for, 75
Geraldo Rivera Live, 107
Gestalt therapy, 99
Goodman, Ariel, 155
Gore, Al, 239
Governor, terms as, 86–87
Gracen, Elizabeth Ward, 39
Grandiose self, 112–113
   regression of, 114–115
Grandiosity, 61, 88
   as coping mechanism, 88–89
   denial and, 236–237
   drug addiction and, 133
Greatness, 117
Group therapy, 204
   private therapy groups, 223–224
Guilt, 204
   homosexual fantasies and, 219–220

H

Harding, Warren, 126
Hart, Gary, 92
Healthy sex, 155–156
Heroes, 59–60, 61
   parentified child, 88
Heterosexual monogamy, 156
Higher power, 185–186
High school years, 70–74
Hit-and-run mentality, 215

Index

Hitting bottom, 182, 183
  job loss as, 209
HIV (human immunodeficiency
    virus), 29, 36, 199–201
Holmes, Oliver Wendell, Jr., xii
Homosexuality, 36–37
  fantasies, homosexual,
    219–220
  military and, 120, 124
  monogamy, 156
  12–step program and,
    189–192
Hot Springs, Arkansas, 53
Humiliating comments, 198

I

The Iceman Cometh (O'Neill),
    31
Idealism, political, 118
Idealization, 111
  of politicians, 126
  primitive idealization, 123
Ideals, 113
Identification with the aggres-
    sor, 82–83
Identity, 125
  diffusion, 125
*I'm Dysfunctional, You're Dys-
    functional* (Kaminer), 66
Impeachment, 21, 146
Impulsive, addictions as, 93–94
Incest, 50
Inconsistency, 124
Indiscretion, 100
Infidelity, 86–87
  Clinton, Virginia and Roger,
    54–55

  of Eisenhower, Dwight D.,
    139
  of Johnson, Lyndon B., 139
  list of Clinton's affairs, 92–93
  rationalizing, 208
  record of, 14
  of Roosevelt, Franklin De-
    lano, 137, 138–139
Inner child, 241
Inpatient therapy, 174, 202
Insecurity, 11–12
Insight therapy, 153
Instability, 119
Integrity
  problem, 238
  of Truman, Harry, 121
Internalizing emotional tasks,
    113
Internal representation of the
    idealized parent, 112–113
Intimacy, 102
Invasiveness of addiction, 33
Isolation
  of affect, 57
  trauma and, 218

J

James, William, 112
Jefferson, Thomas, xiii
Job loss, 209
Johnson, Ladybird, 139
Johnson, Lyndon B., 137
  infidelity of, 139
Jones, Paula Corbin, 10, 39, 94,
    98, 143
  motives of, 106–107
  settlement with, 105–107

Index

K

Kaminer, Wendy, 5, 66–67
Kelly, Virginia, 14–15, 98
  biography of, 44–45
  Clinton, Hillary Rodham
    and, 81–82
  on death of Clinton, Roger, 76
  divorce of, 63
  high school years of Clinton
    and, 73–74
  reconnection, attempts at,
    89–90
  remarriage to Clinton,
    Roger, 63
  resemblance to Lewinsky,
    Monica, 19
  return of, 49–50
  spousal abuse of, 62
Kennedy, John F., 9, 117–118,
  137–138
  resemblance of Clinton to,
    145
  risk-taking behavior of,
    145–146
Khantzian, Edward, 131–132
Kierkegaard, Soren, 159
Kleptomania, 23
  sexual kleptomania, 24, 238
Kohut, Heinz, 111–115
Koresh, David, 159

L

Language, use of, 112
Leadership, 117–118
  instability and, 119
Legal problems, sex-related,
  29–30

Leoporello's "catalogue song,"
  105
Lewinsky, Monica, 5–6, 10, 11,
  12, 13–14, 39
  addictive pattern and, 19
  denial of affair, 167
  Kelly, Virginia, resemblance
    to, 19
  risk and, 143
  sexual advances by Clinton,
    100
  time of involvement with
    Clinton, 98–99
Lewis, Jean, 95
Little Rock, Arkansas, 85–86
Love
  desire for, 109–110
  sex and, 156
Lovelessness, 213
Loyalty program, 121
Lying, 123–124

M

McCarthy, Joseph, 121
McCord, Mr. and Mrs., 104
McGill University, 158
McGovern, George, 118–119
Madison Guaranty Savings and
  Loan, 95
Maimonides, 37
Mandela, Nelson, 125
Manic depression, 154
Manipulation, 123
Maraniss, David, xv, xiv, 4,
  18–19, 19
Mark Antony, 9, 10
Marlatt, Gordon, 204

Marriage to Rodham, Hillary,
84–85
Mascot role, 59
Masturbation, 168, 169–170,
173, 192–193
as biological need, 222–223
homosexual fantasies and,
217–218
Media
and Flowers, Gennifer, 94
privacy and, 142–143
Menninger, Karl, 132
Mercer, Lucy, 138
Methamphetamine, 167–169
Meyers, Wayne, 32–33
Military. *See also* Vietnam War
draft evasion, 16
homosexuals in, 120, 124
Miller, Alice, 76–77, 123
Minimizing, 213
Minnesota Multiphasic Person-
ality Inventory (MMPI),
88
Mirroring, 111
Clinton's need for, 113–114
realistic ambition and, 113
Monogamy, 156–157
Monroe, Marilyn, 9, 146
Moral inventory, 186–187
Moral values
ethics and, 3–4
loss of, 97
Morris, Dick, 120–121
Moses, 159
Motivation of self-destruction,
131, 133
Mourning losses, 234–235

Mozart, 105
Musterbation, 72
My Boss Ike (Summersby), 139
Myth of the cave, 160

N

Narcissism, pathological,
113–114
Narcissistic wound, 197
Narcotics Anonymous (N.A.),
181
National Council on Sexual
Addiction and Compul-
sivity, 24–25
National Institutes of Health,
25
Neurochemistry, 42
New School for Social Re-
search, Manhattan, xi
New York Times, 125, 142
Nietzsche, Friedrich, 4
Nixon, Richard, 12–13, 81
death of, 147–148

O

Objectifying women, 102
Obsessive-compulsive disorder,
154
O'Neill, Eugene, 31
"On the Capacity to Be Alone"
(Winnicott), 69
Oral sex, 87
religion and, 167
The Origins of Alcoholism
(McCord & McCord),
104
O'Shea, Kitty, 9

Out of the Shadows: Understanding Sexual Addiction (Carnes), 24
Outpatient therapy, 174, 204
Overachievers, 60, 77
Overeaters Anonymous (O.A.), 181
Oxford Group, 178
Oxford University, 77–78

P

Panic
  and aloneness, 70
  control and, 161
Panic disorder, 154, 219, 221
Parentified child, 88
Parnell, Charles Stewart, 9, 10
Pathological narcissism, 113–114
Pearls, Fritz, 99
Perot, Ross, 18
Personality, 116
Personality disorder, 205
Pharmacological treatment of addiction, 155
Phobias, 154
Physical impoverishment, 35
Plato, 160
Political policy, 120–122
Political skills, 74
  in high school, 72–73
Polls, reliance on, 120–121
Polyaddiction. *See* Cross-addiction
Popularity, 71
Pornographic videos, 167–170
Portis, Jonathan, xiv

Posttraumatic stress disorder (PTSD), 154, 217–218
  Vietnam War veterans, 230
Power
  abuse of, 135
  addiction to, 60
Powerlessness, 203–204
Pragmatism, 119
Presidential campaign, 1996, 18
Primitive idealization, 123
Prisoners of Childhood (Miller), 77
Private individual therapy, 204–223, 239
Private therapy groups, 223–224
Profiles in Courage (Kennedy), 117–118
Prozac, 155
Pseudointimacy, 102
Pseudorelationships, 102
  trust and, 103
Psychiatric diagnosis, 25–26
Psychodynamic therapy, 153
Psychological determinants, 42
  Clinton, Bill and, 65
Psychopathic deviant scale, 88
Psychotherapy, 153
Psychotic episodes, 231

R

Rabin, Yitzhak, 14–15, 98, 123
  as father figure, 16
  loss of, 16–17
Racial issues, 124
Rage, 98, 201, 204
  dealing with, 235–236

Rage *(continued)*
  outbursts of, 86
  reactions, 199
  rejection and, 216
  sexual addiction and, 199
  shame and, 198
Rageaholics, 48, 51
Rationalizing, 118
  infidelities, 208
Realistic ambition, 113
Reality
  distortion of, 55
  revision of, 101
Reassurance, desire for, 65–66
Recklessness, 100
Recovery, 155, 211
  control and panic, 161
  determination of, 157
  feeling of, 237–238
  reasons for, 234
  shame about, 232–233
Regression, 57
  of grandiose self, 114–115
Reich, Robert, 77–78, 104
Rejection, 200
  rate and, 216
Relapses, 192–193
  prevention, 155, 204
  recovery and, 211
Religion, 166–167
  cults, 159
  sexual addiction and, 172–173
  in 12–step program, 186
"Renascence" (St. Vincent Millay), 184
Repeated sexual activity, 28
Repetition compulsion, 164

Resolution, failure of, 33
Resolution Trust Corporation (RTC), 95
Respectability, 55–56
Responsibility, addiction and, 159–160
Rhodes scholarship, 76
Rice, Donna, 92
Right-wing conspiracy theory, 144
Risk and addiction, 29–30, 143–144
Rodham, Hillary. *See* Clinton, Hillary Rodham
Roles
  in dysfunctional families, 59–60
  women's roles, 140–141
Roosevelt, Anna, 138
Roosevelt, Eleanor, 138
Roosevelt, Franklin Delano, 9, 119
  infidelity of, 137, 138
Rosenthal, A. M., 4, 23
Rutherford, Lucy Mercer, 9

S
Sadness, 204
Safe sex, 201
St. Vincent Millay, Edna, 184
Seduction, 96–97
Seeds of addiction, 130
Self, sense of, 112
Self-destruction, 12–13
  addiction and, 127
  flirting with, 143–144
  geographic cure, 134

motivation of, 131, 132–133
physical death and,
134–135
risk and, 144–145
Self-esteem, 11–12, 104, 204
acting out and, 199–200
narcissistic wound, 197–199
Self-hate, 35, 88
Self-help, 224–233
Self-medication, addiction as,
131–132
Self-pity, 13
Self-punishment, 132
Sensation seekers, 54
Serenity Prayer, 180
Sex, attitudes about, 140
Sex Addicts Anonymous
(S.A.A.), 24, 182
Sexaholics Anonymous (S.A.),
24, 182
Sex and Love Addicts Anony-
mous (S.L.A.A.), 24, 182
Sexual abuse, 50, 164
forgiveness of, 221–222
posttraumatic stress disor-
der (PTSD) and, 218
shame and, 198
Sexual Compulsives Anonymous
(S.C.A.), 24, 155, 172–173,
182, 192–193, 209–210
Sexuality, inappropriate expo-
sure to, 50–51
Sexual kleptomania, 24, 238
Sexually transmitted diseases, 35
HIV (human immunodefi-
ciency virus), 29, 36,
199–201

Sexual Recovery Institute,
24–25
definition of addiction,
26–27
Shame, 97, 125–126, 204
mistreatment and, 198
uncovering shame, 155
Simpson, O. J., 107
60 Minutes, 11
Slavery, addiction as, 158–159
Smith, Bob, 177–179
Smoking, attitudes about,
141–142
Social determinants, 42, 43
Clinton, Bill and, 65
Social/interpersonal problems,
30
Social restraints, 88
Sociopaths, 85, 97
Spanking, 213
Special status, 61
Spirituality, 166, 202
awakening of, 188–189
impoverishment, 35
Starr, Kenneth, 10, 100, 127,
143, 146
Steinem, Gloria, 5
Stevenson, Adlai, xv–xvi
Success, drive for, 72
Summersby, Kay, 139
Superego, 4
Swanson, Gloria, 146

T

Tammany Hall, 126
Teenage years of Clinton, 62
Temper tantrums, 86

Tension, 56–57
Terminal uniqueness, 61–62
  as coping mechanism,
    88–89
Thacker, Ebby, 178–179
Thomas, Dylan, 237
Thomas, Norman, 119
Tolerance of sexual activity,
    30–31
Top-down approaches, 153–154
Transference, 135
Traumatization through omis-
    sion, 114
Triggers, 204
Truman, Harry, 121
Trust, 58
  intimacy and, 103
  pseudorelationships and,
    103
  recovery and, 237
Truthfulness, 123–124
Turning passive into active, 62,
    164
12–step recovery programs, 61,
    66, 153. *See also* Alco-
    holics Anonymous (A.A.)
  principles of, 182–189
Tyrrell, R. Emmett, Jr., xiv–xv

U

Unconditional love, 110
Undocumented workers, 120
University of Arkansas, Fayet-
    teville, 81
Unprotected sex, 28–29

V

Values, 113
Vietnam War, 78
  draft evasion, 16
  veterans, trauma of, 226–230
Vulnerability of Clinton, 93

W

Watergate scandal, 81
Welfare reform bill, 1996, 119
Wells, Orson, 60
Whitewater issue, 95
Willey, Kathleen, 39, 95–97, 98
  denial of charges, 101
  risk and, 143
Willpower, 203–204
Wilson, Bill, 177–179
Winnicott, Donald, 69, 89
Withdrawal
  decision-making during, 187
  symptoms of, 32–33
Women's roles, 140–141
Woods, Kimba, 120
Working through theory,
    91–92
World Health Organization
    (WHO), 38
Wright, Betsey, 92–93, 105

Y

Yale University, 78–79

Z

Zelig, 125
Zuckerman, Marvin, 54